POLITICAL SOCIALIZATION

STUDIES IN BEHAVIORAL POLITICAL SCIENCE

Series editor Robert Presthus

Other series volumes in preparation

POLITICAL VALUES OF AMERICAN PHYSICAL
  SCIENTISTS, *Vaughn Blankenship*
CONSEQUENCES OF INFLUENCE IN INTERNATIONAL
  POLITICS, *Raymond Tanter*
THE JUDICIAL MIND RE-VISITED, *Glendon Schubert*
INTEREST GROUP BEHAVIOR IN CANADA AND
  THE UNITED STATES, *Robert Presthus*

POLITICAL

SOCIALIZATION

 KENNETH P. LANGTON

The University of Michigan

New York

Oxford University Press

London 1969 *Toronto*

To My Parents

FOREWORD

The field of political science is clearly becoming more systematic, in terms of theoretical orientations as well as research methods. The emerging tendency in graduate programs to separate theory into normative-historical and data-organizing, heuristic segments suggests the ubiquity of this trend. In the process, many of us have felt some need to recast our concepts of the discipline and, in some cases, to acquaint ourselves with methods which have in the past been more characteristic of sociology and psychology than of our own discipline. *Studies in Behavioral Political Science* is essentially an attempt to ease this process by providing several examples of behavioral research and the theoretical frameworks within which it occurs. We have tried to encompass the various subareas of the discipline, using a variety of methods ranging from rather traditional survey analysis to fairly sophisticated computer techniques. In every case the authors have attempted to make their theory and operation explicit. Our second objective has been to contribute new substantive knowledge.

Kenneth Langton's comparative study in political socialization, the first book in this series, informs both objectives. Using a sample of Jamaican families, plus data from a national survey of high-school students in the United States, he demonstrates the utility of behavioral methods while adding to our knowledge of the conditions under which children acquire their political norms. Family structure, peer group, sex, and social class are among the variables used to explain differences in this process. Finally, Langton specifies certain policy implications for programs of civic education in democratic societies. Our hope is that his careful study, as well as subsequent volumes in the series, will prove useful to our colleagues.

Robert Presthus

January 1969
Toronto

PREFACE

The major focus of this book is on the influence of different social agencies in the political socialization process. Because of the need for theoretically compelling questions capable of being tested in diverse political cultures, I have made this study as cross-cultural in its orientation as the data and literature will allow.

While information is drawn from a number of sources, the major ones are a national sample of Jamaican students in government-aided secondary schools collected in spring, 1964, and a national sample of American high school seniors conducted by the Survey Research Center, University of Michigan, in spring, 1965. A sample of 1349 school children from Detroit, Michigan, is used for comparative purposes in Chapter 5. Although both national samples are of adolescents in secondary schools, the analysis reflects potentially on a much broader span of the life cycle.

Jamaica is similar to other societies in transition to industrialization, which together include well over half of the world's population. Although primarily agrarian, Jamaica is striving for industrial expansion and economic development, at the same time coping with population pressure, unemployment, and illiteracy. Important changes are occurring in the distribution of economic and political power, and in traditional norms and values.

Since 1944, there has been a relatively stable transfer of power within a well-established two-party system and a peaceful transition from colonial rule to independent self-government. These developments have been greatly influenced by those who hold positions of power and prestige in various social institutions: government, business, education, labor, and so forth. It is important to ask in what manner future leaders and citizens are being socialized to accept their roles within the political system.

As the secondary school is one of the most important recruitment channels into the active citizenry and leadership in Jamaica (as in many less-industrialized countries), a study of the political socialization of the secondary school population will be of manifest political interest.

Although the twelfth grader in the United States is not in so exclusive a recruitment channel as his peers in less-industrialized countries, he is, like his Jamaican counterpart, at a significant juncture. He is approaching the point when he will leave his parents' family, and thus their future political influence will be less. The adolescent is also nearing the end of his high school experience, which for the majority of non-college bound students means the end of their formal civics education. Because he has yet to establish marriage and occupational ties, each with its potential patterns of influence, this is an important stage in his life in which to assess the influence of present and past socialization agencies.

While the questions raised in this study, it is hoped, will have sufficient conceptual scope to be relevant in many national cultures, the study's orientation is essentially empirical. The modes of analyses proceed in the early chapters from an uncomplicated examination of controlled contingency tables, to multi-variate analysis, to a form of causal modeling in Chapter 6 which may prove useful in answering some of the more difficult substantive and methodological questions facing students of political socialization.

The study is reported in seven parts. The first part is introductory and places the research in the context of socialization, raising the conceptual questions which provide the broad guidelines for the remaining chapters.

Chapters 2 through 6 present the body of data. Chapter 2 scrutinizes the indirect influence of family structure to determine its effect on politically relevant variables. Since the constancy of these resultant attitudes over the life cycle of the individual should not be treated as a premise, the quasi-longitudinal sample design used in the Caribbean enables us to make inferences concerning their stability over time. In the final part of Chapter 2, the political impact of family structure in the Caribbean is contrasted with that in the United States.

Chapter 3 continues to focus on the family, but examines the relative influences of mother and father in *directly* transmitting their political orientations to their children. Although the investigation centers essentially on relative parental influence in the United States, comparisons are made with the Caribbean data in the concluding section of the chapter.

Chapters 4 and 5 turn from the family to such secondary agencies as the peer group and school. Chapter 4 assesses the role of the formal school environment on political learning, while Chapter 5 examines the informal milieu of the peer group and school.

Chapter 6 seeks to integrate some of the earlier concerns with individual agencies as it incorporates the three institutions—family, peer group, and school—within a single causal model to assess their relative impact on the political socialization process. Chapter 7 summarizes the study in a conceptual context, treats some of its limitations, and examines the implications of political socialization research for the implementation of values in the political system.

From 1963, when I realized that the study of political socialization was one of the more important routes to understanding how and why people act politically, I have accumulated a formidable number of debts.

Philip E. Converse and James C. Davies provided valuable critiques on drafts of some of the earlier chapters; and I benefited from the helpful comments of John Kingdon, who read the entire manuscript. In particular, I wish to express my appreciation to M. Kent Jennings, who as a friend, collaborator, and colleague has been singularly generous in his assistance and advice.

Thanks also go to Robert Presthus for his thoughtful editorial advice, to Laura Johnson for her careful editing, and to James Anderson of Oxford University Press. The editors and publishers of *The American Political Science Review, The Journal of Politics,* and *The Western Political Quarterly* have permitted me to revise and reprint material which appeared in their journals. Financial support has been provided by the United States Office of Education and the National Institute of Mental Health.

It is a pleasure to thank my wife, Joanne, for her constant assistance, enthusiastic support, and the non-political socialization of our two children in their father's frequent absence.

K.P.L.

Ann Arbor, Michigan
January 1969

CONTENTS

LIST OF TABLES

TABLE

FIGURES

POLITICAL SOCIALIZATION

CHAPTER ONE

THE STUDY OF
POLITICAL SOCIALIZATION

¦¦¦¦¦¦ The occurrence of patterned behavior among individuals is well-documented in social research. Students respond to cultural cues by continually electing their class officers by majority vote; children obey the commands of the traffic policeman; adults consistently vote for the Republican Party or accept as "legitimate" John F. Kennedy's assumption of office in 1960 after a very close election. All are examples of this type of behavior. Such patterns may well be interpreted in terms of contemporary influences in the lives of particular individuals or groups. However, the continuity of many patterns over time and place suggests that the individual has been modified in the course of his development in such a way so that he often exhibits persistent behavior apart from the momentary effect of his immediate environment. This behavior results from the socialization process: an individual's learning from others in his environment the social patterns and values of his culture.

The study of socialization is not a new field. Such inquiries have been prominent in social psychology, anthropology, and psychiatry, yet the investigation of political behavior as a consequence of socialization is relatively new. This does not mean that those interested in politics have not been aware of its importance. "Citizenship" training and civic socialization are strongly emphasized in Plato's *Republic*, Aristotle's *Politics*, and Rousseau's *Emile*. However, only in recent years have the results of empirical investigations about the relations between the socialization process and political behavior begun to appear in the literature.[1]

Political Socialization: A Definition

Most attempts to define socialization have generally agreed that it is a process in which individuals incorporate into their own attitudinal structure and behavior patterns the ways of their respective social groups and society. John Whiting and Irvin Child describe this in more colorful terms:

> In all societies the helpless infant, getting his food by nursing at his mother's breast and, having digested it, freely evacuating the waste products, exploring his genitals, biting and kicking at will, must be changed into a responsible adult obeying the rules of his society.[2]

Political socialization, in the broadest sense, refers to the way society transmits its political culture from generation to generation. This process may serve to preserve traditional political norms and institutions; on the other hand, when secondary socialization agencies inculcate political values different from those of the past or when children are raised with political and social expectations different from those of

---

[1] For a review of much of this literature see John J. Patrick, "Political Socialization of American Youth: A Review of Research with Implications for Secondary School Social Studies," High School Curriculum Center in Government, Indiana University, Bloomington, Indiana, March, 1967; Stephen L. Wasby, "The Impact of the Family on Politics: An Essay and Review of the Literature," *Family Life Coordinator*, 15 (January, 1966), 3–23; Richard E. Dawson, "Political Socialization," in James A. Robinson (ed.), *Political Science Annual: An International Review*, Vol. I (Indianapolis: Bobbs-Merrill, 1966), pp. 1–84; and Jack Dennis, "Recent Research on Political Socialization: A Bibliography of Published, Forthcoming, and Unpublished Works, Theses, and Dissertations and a Survey of Projects in Progress," prepared for the Theory and Research Working Committee on Political Socialization of the Council on Civic Education, Lincoln Filene Center for Citizenship and Public Affairs, Tufts University, Medford, Massachusetts, 1967.

[2] John W. Whiting and Irvin L. Child, *Child Training and Personality: A Cross Cultural Study* (New Haven: Yale University Press, 1963), p. 63.

their forebears, the socialization process can be a vehicle of political and social change.

For our purposes we shall view political socialization as the process, mediated through various agencies of society, by which an individual learns politically relevant attitudinal dispositions and behavior patterns. These agencies include such environmental categories as the family, peer group, school, adult organizations, and the mass media. The role of each has been stressed in the literature. This list of categories, of course, is not exhaustive, for example, class, sex, and age sub-cultures might also be included.

Although specifying relevant attitudinal, cognitive, and evaluational categories still provides the core of research in political science, theory-building and research have developed sufficiently to indicate the following as examples of relevant areas of focus: attitudes and behavior related to political legitimacy, electoral behavior, interest articulation, decision-making which affects the authoritative allocation of values in the system, feelings of personal competency to influence decisions affecting the allocation of values, and attitudes toward authority. Thus the concept of political socialization is as broad in its empirical referents as those aspects of social behavior that can be meaningfully related to politics.

Political Conceptualization and Political Socialization

Political scientists have offered various schemes that attempt to provide some conceptual basis for the organization and delimitation of political socialization research. But contemporary research has yet to produce an agreed-upon model for this analysis. Most of the different frameworks are classification schemes, which on closer examination seem to cover similar portions of the same landscape.[3] Yet they have brought

[3] For critiques of finished works and general conceptual and stock-taking efforts see Fred Greenstein, "Political Socialization," *International Encyclopedia of the Social Sciences* (New York: Crowell Collier, forthcoming); Roberta Sigel, "Political Socialization: Some Reactions on Current Approaches and Conceptualizations," paper presented at the

a necessary measure of direction to the study of political socialization at this early stage in its development.

The model most heralded for its parsimonious yet comprehensive format is one by David Easton and Robert Hess, which grew out of Easton's previous work in general systems theory.[4] An input-output conversion model is basic to Easton's view of the political system. "Inputs" include both demands and supports. One means by which the system supports or maintains itself is by way of political socialization. Every political system, if it is to survive, must to some degree develop supportive expectations among its members. Easton suggests a three-tier classification of political phenomena toward which political socialization is directed, including the government, regime, and political community. Government includes those authorities who are the day-to-day occupants of the more important political decision-making roles in society. Regime refers to the rules of the political game (e.g., majority rule) which legitimate and determine the character of authoritative roles, as well as specify what is expected of citizens or subjects. Political community is something akin to shared national identity. Viewed through this conceptual prism, the primary task of the student of socialization is to explain how the political socialization process has a disruptive or supportive influence on each level of the political system.

Structural functionalists approach socialization as Easton does, but with a different emphasis. They see political and social systems as performing requisite functions necessary for their maintenance. Talcott Parsons, for example, postulates

Annual Meeting of the American Political Science Association, New York, September, 1966; Richard Dawson and Kenneth Prewitt, *Aspects of Political Socialization* (Boston: Little, Brown, 1969); and Jack Dennis, "Major Problems of Political Socialization Research," *Midwest Journal of Political Science*, 12 (February, 1968), 85–114.

[4] David Easton and Robert Hess, "Youth and The Political System," in S. M. Lipset and L. Lowenstein (eds.), *Cultural and Social Character* (New York: Free Press, 1961), pp. 226–51. See also Easton, "An Approach to the Analysis of Political Systems," *World Politics*, 9 (1957), 383–400; and *A Systems Analysis of Political Life* (New York: Wiley, 1965).

four such functions, one of which is "pattern maintenance."[5] This involves the maintenance of conformity to the prescriptions of the cultural system. Through the socialization process, individuals are molded into wanting to fulfill role expectations of the society and polity.

Using a similar structural-functional perspective, William C. Mitchell focuses specifically on the political system.[6] Like Parsons, he postulates requisite system functions and, like Easton, he views the system as essentially an input-output conversion process. The "integration of the political system," one of the four functions, includes the formal and informal processes of socialization. Political socialization not only affects the inputs into the polity, such as demands, resources, and support, but also affects the "processes" by which inputs are converted into decisional outputs.

The conceptualization of Gabriel Almond and Sidney Verba is closely related to that of Parsons and Mitchell.[7] Almond produces a set of seven requisite functional categories for the analysis of Western and non-Western systems and, like Easton, he divides these into input and output processes. Among the four input functions which must be performed by all political systems he includes political socialization. This process is seen as largely determining the stability of "political culture" and structures over time.

Fred Greenstein has attempted to combine several of the basic elements in the various conceptual formulations into a series of questions pertaining to political socialization.[8] His five basic questions are essentially a restatement of Lasswell's

[5] Talcott Parsons and Neil Smelser, *Economy and Society* (Glencoe, Ill.: Free Press, 1956), pp. 16–17. Also see W. C. Mitchell, *Sociological Analysis and Politics* (Englewood Cliffs, N.J.: Prentice-Hall, 1967), pp. 82, 123–24.

[6] William C. Mitchell, *The American Polity* (Glencoe: Free Press, 1962), chap. 7.

[7] Gabriel Almond and James S. Coleman, *The Politics of the Developing Area* (Princeton: Princeton University Press, 1960), pp. 3–64; and Gabriel Almond and Sidney Verba, *The Civic Culture* (Princeton: Princeton University Press, 1963).

[8] Fred Greenstein, *Children and Politics* (New Haven: Yale University Press, 1965), p. 12.

formulation of the general process of communication: "(a) who (b) learns what (c) from whom (d) under what circumstances (e) with what effects."[9]

A distinction is often made between a macro, or "system level," approach to socialization and an individual approach. The former focuses, for example, on the role or function political socialization plays in the stabilization, change, and integration, of political systems. The latter supposedly emphasizes the process whereby an individual acquires political orientations. While this distinction may be an apt description of the gap between empirical research and contemporary political conceptualization in the socialization area, it is somewhat artificial, and a combined focus is necessary if we are to develop empirically based analytical theory.[10] While current macro-conceptualization is important for the questions it raises and the direction it provides, the history of the first empirically based analytical theory in political science is likely to have its strongest roots in the more humble inductive process.

Study of Political Socialization

Political socialization is basically a continuous social and psychological process composed of four elements. It involves (1) an interaction-acquisition process, (2) between the individual being socialized, (3) the agency which acts as the vehicle of socialization, and (4) the political behavior patterns, perceptions, and attitudes which he learns. The problems facing the students of socialization center on these four elements.

Socialization Process

Many different non-political conceptual frameworks have been advanced to explain the interaction-acquisition process by which socialization occurs. Some are based on the study of the maladjusted, others have their roots in the study of

[9] See Mitchell, *The American Polity*, p. 146, for a similar set of questions.

[10] For an excellent description and discussion of the properties and function of an empirically based analytical theory see Warren S. Torgerson, *Theory and Methods of Scaling* (New York: Wiley, 1958), chap. 1.

primitive people, others in highly controlled laboratory experiments on animals and children, and still others on the study and observation of "normal" children and adults in primarily Western societies. Considering the varied perspectives and sources of information, differences in interpretation are not surprising. So far, no one approach has received general acceptance.[11] In this section we shall discuss briefly three of the major approaches to socialization: learning, personality, and role.

Although each of these approaches sets different problems for itself and has different orientations, to a considerable extent the approaches are complementary—as will be seen when role theory is discussed. All three assume that an individual acquires behavioral predispositions in the course of social interaction, and that such social patterns are not likely to be acquired and reinforced unless they are in some way gratifying.

Learning, as used by psychologists, is a broad term applying to all behavior which derives from training procedures.[12] Many learning theorists view behavior in terms of measurable stimuli and responses and attempt to determine the principles by which they are linked. This linkage is usually explained by the concepts of conditioning and reinforcement. If the socializing agent wishes, for example, to control or direct a child's behavior, he must make clear the distinction between old and new behavior patterns. "Cues" must be provided to

[11] See William H. Sewell, "Some Recent Developments in Socialization Theory and Research," *The Annals of the American Academy,* 349 (September, 1963), 163–81; and Frederick Elkin, *The Child and Society* (New York: Random House, 1960), for a discussion of different theoretical approaches to the study of socialization.

[12] Ernest R. Hilgard, *Theories of Learning* (New York: Appleton, 1960) 2nd ed.; Neal E. Miller and John Dollard, *Social Learning and Imitation* (New Haven: Yale University Press, 1941); and William E. Martin and Celia B. Stendler, *Child Behavior and Development* (New York: Harcourt, 1959 rev.).

Robert Hess and Judith Torney have proposed that different types of political learning involve several different learning models. See *The Development of Political Attitudes in Children* (Chicago: Aldine, 1967), pp. 19–22.

clarify the situations in which the new behavior is expected and those in which it is not. Rewards and punishments are said to "reinforce" the desired behavior patterns. The effectiveness of such reinforcement increases (1) the more often and consistently "correct" behavior is rewarded and (2) the sooner the reward comes after the correct behavior.

An important concept in explaining socialization is imitation, a response pattern which occurs under given conditions as a result of the learning process.[13] A young child usually learns early that life is more rewarding if he follows in the footsteps of the older and more powerful people with whom he interacts. In order to gratify his needs he may form the habit of imitating the people upon whom he is dependent. Behavior which is rewarded is reinforced, that which is not is dropped.

Often incidental cues will lead to "correct" imitative behavior. A child seeking parental attention may hear his father announcing proudly that he is a Republican, his father and father's father were Republicans, and any honest and decent man could not be anything but a Republican—an obvious cue. The child responds by announcing that he is a Republican, and is rewarded by receiving attention. Judging from this well-structured situation, parental attention will not be negative. To the extent that the child repeats this strategy to gain attention he has learned new behavior. However, at this stage in the socialization process, the child's imitation of parental party preference probably occurs without regard to the complexity of values and beliefs that may be related to the parent's partisan preference.

Imitation is closely related to the process of identification in which the child, or older individual for that matter, tries to *be* another person. There are different views concerning the basis for identification: Some psychologists believe that the youngster identifies first with the person who gratifies his needs, others believe that he identifies with the person whose status he envies and who withholds from him the things he

[13] Neal Miller and John Dollard, *Social Learning and Imitation* (New Haven: Yale University Press, 1941).

wants.[14] In any case, the child, consciously or unconsciously, begins to identify with the important "other" individual and to internalize his attitudes as well as to imitate his behavior. Identification usually begins within the family where parents are taken as models. As the child matures he takes other referents for his behavior: peers, teachers, and work group members; next he might take persons outside his immediate environment—imaginary as well as real—such as historical figures.

Identification may represent a more advanced stage in the formation of political party identification. In this process the individual is not only imitating behavior but internalizing attitudes often associated with party preference, for example, attitudes toward government ownership. How much the individual identifies and internalizes related attitudes may determine the stability over time of his partisan identification.

Since research in learning has been developed largely under laboratory conditions, it is ordinarily more controlled and methodologically precise than personality or social-role research. While it has provided many insights to students of socialization, it has been less than successful in explaining social situations which involve complex motivations and ambivalent feelings.

Turning to personality and role approaches, there has been considerable discussion as to the relative influence of personality versus the situation, or role, in orienting behavior. Clearly, some situations are highly structured, and the social norms are so unambiguous that personality differences have a limited effect on behavior. On the other hand, less structured situations may afford greater scope for the psychological dispositions to affect behavior.[15] It would rarely seem to be an

[14] Jerome Kagan, "The Concept of Identification," *Psychological Review*, 65 (September, 1958), 296–305; Urie Bronfenbrenner, "Freudian Theories of Identification and Their Derivatives," *Child Development*, 31 (1958), 15–40; and Roger Burton and John Whiting, "The Absent Father and Cross-Sex Identity," *Merrill-Palmer Quarterly*, 7 (April, 1961), 84–95.

[15] For an important discussion of personality and politics see Fred Greenstein, "The Impact of Personality on Politics: An Attempt to

"either-or" proposition with its simple but implicit view of the bivariate or single-dimensional nature of causality. Rather, as Figure 1.1. suggests, a multi-variate model, which combines to some degree both types of explanation, seems closer to reality.

To the extent that socialization research focuses on the relations between social institutions and attitudinal dispositions or personality,[16] it should be remembered that the relevance of these attitudes is determined by their relations to politically meaningful behavior.[17] Much literature has concerned itself with the connections between social institutions and attitudes[18] and between attitudes and behavior.[19] Un-

---

Clear Away Underbrush," *American Political Science Review*, 61 (September, 1967), 629–41.

[16] Those who wish to review how the insights of the psychoanalytical school have been incorporated into the socialization literature should see Sigmund Freud, *An Outline of Psychoanalysis* (London: Hogarth Press, 1949); and Talcott Parsons and Robert Bales, *Family, Socialization and Interaction Process* (Glencoe: Free Press, 1965).

For a discussion of psychoanalytical propositions that have been subjected to empirical tests see Harold Orlansky, "Infant Care and Personality," *Psychological Bulletin*, 46 (January, 1949), 1–48; Whiting and Child, *Child Training and Personality;* and Irvin L. Child, "Socialization," in Gardner Lindzey (ed.), *Handbook of Social Psychology* (Cambridge: Addison-Wesley, 1954), 655–92.

[17] Those who are not interested in the development of empirically based analytical theory may disagree with this statement. Certainly, if one argues normatively that the whole point of establishing and maintaining governmental structure is to meet the needs of the governed, then one can also maintain that their affective attitudes regarding governmental output, and so forth, may have "political" relevance aside from their relationship to behavior.

On the other hand, a behavioral criterion does not mean that a map of mass legitimacy attitudes, for example, would not have political significance in time one; but this is dependent to a major degree on whether it can be used to explain and predict future behavior—either on the part of the masses or the leadership—in time two. The need for more longitudinal studies to test the relevance of what appear to be manifestly political attitudes is obvious.

[18] For example, Fred J. Greenstein, "The Benevolent Leader: Children's Images of Political Authority," *American Political Science Review*, 54 (December, 1960), 934–44; Robert D. Hess and David Easton, "The Child's Changing Image of the President," *Public Opinion Quarter-*

fortunately, there has been little research which has attempted to connect all three: the environmental agency to the psychological disposition and the disposition to politically relevant behavior (linkages A and B in Figure 1.1). If we find, for instance, that feelings of personal political efficacy are related to political behavior, we must also ask how these attitudes are formed, and investigate the socialization agencies which are important in the process.

Lewis Froman has argued that including attitudinal dispositions as intervening variables in the study of socialization is conceptually important for several reasons. First, this intervening factor is immediately necessary in situations where the environmental stimuli appear to be the same but behavior is different or, conversely, environments are different but behavior is the same. Second, this may lead to more parsimonious theories to the extent that explanations of behavior can be funneled through a smaller number of psychological dispositions rather than be dependent on a more complex environment. Finally, to the degree that inclusion of attitudinal dispositions illuminates the linkage between environmental agencies and behavior, the predictive value of the socialization theories will be enhanced. Equally important, their explanatory power will be increased.[20] It has been argued that the

---

ly, 24 (Winter, 1960), 632–44; Martin L. Levin, "Social Climates and Political Socialization," *Public Opinion Quarterly*, 25 (Winter, 1961), 596–606; David Riesman, *The Lonley Crowd* (New Haven: Yale University Press, 1950), pp. 107–11; Robert E. Lane, *Political Life* (Glencoe: Free Press, 1959), Sect. 4.

[19] Harold D. Lasswell, "The Selective Effect of Personality on Political Participation," in R. Christie and M. Jahoda (eds.), *Studies in the Scope and Method of the Authoritarian Personality* (Glencoe: Free Press, 1954); pp. 197–266; Robert E. Lane, "Political Analysis," and Angus Campbell, Gerald Gurin, and Warren E. Miller, "Political Efficacy and Political Participation," in Heinz Eulau, Samuel J. Eldersveld, and Morris Janowitz (eds.), *Political Behavior* (Glencoe: Free Press, 1959), pp. 115–25, 170–74; and Lester W. Milbrath, "Predispositions Toward Political Contention," *Western Political Quarterly*, 13 (March, 1960), 5–18.

[20] Lewis A. Froman, Jr., "Personality and Political Socialization," *The Journal of Politics*, 23 (May, 1961), 348–49.

inability to explain discovered relationships has been one of the major weaknesses of those conceptual approaches which attempt to show direct linkage between environment and behavior.

While Froman's argument for including personality dispositions in socialization research is persuasive, the political relevance of personality is less than universal. In some studies the correlation between such dispositions and behavior has been found to be very weak, and in other cases negative.[21]

A role theorist would be more inclined to see individual behavior as regulated by socio-cultural ideas of appropriateness. Associated with every position in society is a set of expectations, or role, shared by members of a particular group. Conformity to these role expectations, as they persist or change from situation to situation, determines human behavior.[22] Thus the concept of role serves as a bridge between the person and society. Role is related to the individual to the extent that he internalizes appropriate attitudes and behavior,

[21] Katz and Benjamin found that supposedly racially prejudiced "authoritarians were actually more deferential to Negroes than were non-authoritarians." The finding, the authors felt, was due to a "potentially punitive environment." Irwin Katz and Lawrence Benjamin, "Effects of White Authoritarianism in Biracial Work Groups," *Journal of Abnormal and Social Psychology*, 61 (November, 1960), 448–56. Also see: Rufus Browning and Herbert Jacob, "Power Motivation and the Political Personality," *Public Opinion Quarterly*, 28 (Spring, 1964), 75–90; and Angus Campbell *et al.*, *The American Voter* (New York: Wiley, 1960).

[22] Talcott Parsons deserves major credit for the impetus given to the development of role theory in his attempt to produce a conceptual scheme for the analysis of the structure and process of social systems, focusing on the system of institutionalized roles. *The Social System* (Glencoe: Free Press, 1951). His position is further elaborated in his writings on family structure and the socialization of the child, which presents a detailed analysis of the child's internalization of roles as he passes through various stages of psychosexual development and integration into the family system. See Talcott Parsons and Robert F. Bales, *Family Socialization and the Interaction Process* (Glencoe: Free Press, 1955). For a more recent discussion of role learning and socialization see Orville Brim, Jr., and Stanton Wheeler, *Socialization After Childhood: Two Essays* (New York: Wiley, 1966).

and it is related to society in that particular group expectations exist—however ambiguously. Sets of reciprocal expectations exist regulating the behavior of individuals toward each other depending on their positions in the system. One learns these requirements by interacting with others in a variety of social situations and by gradually developing the ability to take the role of the other.

The relations between the role expectations of a group (agency) and the behavior of an individual, however, is dependent upon a complex linkage (Figure 1.1). Conforming or deviant behavior will be affected by the degree of role consensus within the group, the communication of this expectation, and the individual's reception to or knowledge of the communicated role expectations. An individual already possesses certain psychological dispositions that may be very

FIGURE 1.1. Personality and Role: A Linkage Model

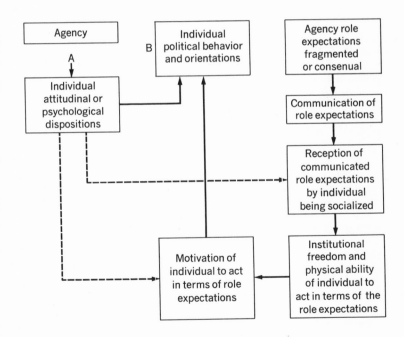

important in determining the level and nature of this receptivity.[23] Other intervening factors include the individual's institutional freedom and physical ability to act in terms of the communicated role expectations, as well as his motivation to act accordingly.[24] Again we see the potential for psychological dispositions affecting the level of motivation.

In the area of socialization, the task of role analysis is to explain how an individual learns to recognize relevant status positions, how he learns to internalize the expectations surrounding these positions, and how he learns to perform appropriately. The possibility for the integration of learning and personality research is manifest.

Agencies and Causal Models

Among the various potential vehicles of political socialization, the family has received by far the greatest attention. In fact, in the past students of socialization have been criticized for their almost exclusive concentration on the family and the experiences of childhood.[25] A danger of this narrow focus is the temptation to generalize too easily from childhood experiences to adult political attitudes and behavior. The major body of literature, which related early family training to adult political behavior, comes from the "national character" school. This group was concerned with finding the dominant psychological patterns within societies—personality patterns which were developed in primary groups and came to characterize

[23] Leon Festinger, *A Theory of Cognitive Dissonance* (New York: Harper & Row, 1957). N. Chapanis and A. Chapanis, "Cognitive Dissonance: Five Years Later," *Psychological Bulletin*, 61 (1964), 1–22; and Milton J. Rosenberg, "An Analysis of Affective-Cognitive Consistency," in M. J. Rosenberg *et al.* (eds.), *Attitude Organization and Change* (New Haven: Yale University Press, 1960), pp. 22 ff. The reader should also note that psychological dispositions possessed by socialization *agents* may also affect their role expectations and the communication of these expectations.

[24] Edgar Borgatta, "Role-Playing Specification, Personality, and Performance," *Sociometry*, 24 (1961), 218–33; Erving Goffman, *Encounters: Two Studies in the Sociology of Interaction* (Indianapolis: Bobbs-Merrill, 1961).

[25] Richard Fagen, *International Politics and Cuba* (forthcoming).

the "modal" person in that society. These different modal personalities resulted in different national political styles in later life. Thus the source of German attitudes toward governmental authority was said to derive from authority patterns in the family: Germans, who were raised in authoritarian families, wanted and expected their political leaders to maintain a similar authoritarian relationship toward them.[26]

When we examine primary socialization agencies, such as the family, to determine their influence upon what appear to be politically relevant attitudes and behavior, we usually try to select and measure what we believe will be pervasive, reasonably enduring attitudinal dimensions and behavior. Certainly family authority patterns may have an important effect on an individual's attitude toward political authority, particularly in less politically developed societies.[27] The authority patterns in the family provide his first exposure to authority. It is also likely that his first view of the political system, even in more structurally differentiated societies, may represent a generalization from these experiences.[28] Yet to think of the political system as the family writ large is too simple.

Early socialization experiences condition an individual's attitudes and role expectations and therefore may affect his

[26] Bertram Schaffner, *Fatherland: A Study of Authoritarianism in the German Family* (New York: Columbia University Press, 1948); and David Rodnick, *Postwar Germans* (New Haven: Yale University Press, 1948); Geoffrey Gorer, *The People of Great Russia* (London: Cresset Press, 1949); and Geoffrey Gorer, *The American People* (New York: Norton, 1948). For a discussion of the "national character" school: see Margaret Mead, "The Study of National Character," in Daniel Learner and Harold D. Lasswell (eds.), *The Policy Sciences* (Stanford: Stanford University Press, 1951), pp. 70–85, and Sidney Verba, *Small Groups and Political Behavior* (Princeton: Princeton University Press), chap. 2.

[27] Robert LeVine, "Political Socialization and Cultural Change," in G. Geertz (ed.), *Old Societies and New States* (New York: Free Press, 1963), pp. 280–303. LeVine makes a more cautious attempt to relate family authority patterns to attitudes toward governmental authority in the East African kingdom of Buganda.

[28] Hess and Easton, "Child's Changing Image," explain that the child's first image of the President represents a generalization from family experience, but the child begins to differentiate between political and family roles as he grows older.

political behavior. However, numerous other factors may intervene between these earliest experiences and later political behavior, greatly inhibiting the impact of the former upon the latter. Orville Brim draws our attention to the difficulty of assuming attitudinal stability from situation to situation.[29] Edwin Levy points out the utility of making some socialization variables more specific to the situations they intend to predict, i.e., for some variables at least, we should study socialization separately within roles.[30]

The same situation may prevail regarding attitude and behavior constancy over time. In their study of the stability of passive and dependent behavior, Jerome Kagan and Howard Moss took repeated measurements of the "dependency trait" in the same group of individuals—measurements which began at the age of three and continued into the late twenties. The most notable feature of their findings is the absence of continuity in this trait. Children who are dependent at age three and four are not the same individuals who emerge as dependent adults.[31]

The first and obvious point is that investigators of the political socialization process cannot make a priori assumptions about the stability over the life cycle of psychological dispositions and political orientations found in childhood. This does not mean that the only correlations we can hope for between socialization practices and attitudes (or behavior) are at one point in time. It is, of course, probable that with a longitudinal or quasi-longitudinal research design, and with the proper experimental or statistical controls on early socialization environments, the lingering effects of this environment on selected dependent variables can be traced over a sig-

[29] Orville Brim, "Personality Development as Role Learning," in I. Iscoe and H. Stevenson (eds.), *Personality Development in Children* (Austin: University of Texas Press, 1960), pp. 127–59; and Brim and Stanton, *Socialization After Childhood: Two Essays.*

[30] Edwin Levy, "Children's Behavior under Stress and its Relation to Training by Parents to Respond to Stress Situations," *Child Development,* 30 (1959), 307–24.

[31] Jerome Kagan and Howard Moss, "The Stability of Passive and Dependent Behavior from Childhood through Adulthood," *Child Development,* 31 (September, 1960), 577–91.

nificant part or the whole life cycle of the individual.[32] But the important point is that the constancy of early socialized attitudes and behavior over the lifetime of an individual must be treated as a researchable question rather than a premise.

Thus, the step from early family socialization to adult political attitudes and behavior is a long one and, as will be suggested, can be fully understood only in terms of the intervening effects of secondary institutions.

The error of some early students of political socialization was their narrow focus on the family. This caused them to exclude such important intermediary institutions as the peer group, school, and work group, as well as the host of adult organizations to which an individual can belong. These organizations and groups play important roles as reinforcing agents of social patterns developed earlier, or they may serve as agencies for re-socialization.

The stability of social patterns over generations is testimony to the reinforcement function. The cumulative impact of membership in a series of social institutions with homogeneous class environments, for instance, may play an important reinforcing role in the socialization process.[33]

Re-socialization takes place when individuals are inducted into new statuses for which no role models previously existed in the society. Most pre-industrial political systems undergoing rapid social change are faced with burdensome tasks of re-socialization.[34] The literature on totalitarian political systems

[32] In the present study, a quasi-longitudinal design and statistical controls are utilized to study the lingering effect of early family socialization on relevant political attitudes over the secondary school experience (see Chapter 2).

[33] See Chapter 5 for a discussion of the influence of homogeneous class environments in schools and peer groups. Also see E. Digby Baltzell, *Philadelphia Gentleman: The Making of a National Upper Class* (New York: Free Press, 1958).

[34] Lucian W. Pye, "Communications and Civic Training in Transitional Societies," in Lucian Pye (ed.), *Communications and Political Development,* (Princeton: Princeton University Press, 1963), pp. 124–27; and "The Stages of Socialization: The Problem of Nation Building," in Joseph Fiszman (ed.), *The American Political Arena* (Boston: Little, Brown, 1966), pp. 84–87.

has also devoted considerable attention to this subject.[35] Another form of re-socialization takes place when a group inducts an individual into a status for which role models previously existed in the society but for which he was not prepared by his earlier training. Social mobility would be a case in point.[36]

Only when the socialization role of these secondary or intermediary institutions is understood will we be able to explain with more confidence why the "well-trained" generation leads a revolution against the established order, or why the radical Japanese adolescent becomes a conservative adult.

While the specific roles of such primary and secondary socialization agencies as the family and school have provided the basis for considerable research, the more comprehensive question of the *relative* influence of each of the major socialization agencies has been largely avoided. This question, as much as any other, represents the substantive and methodological frontier of political socialization research. The model in Figure 1.2 indicates the various causal linkages, the relative importance of which must be determined if we are to understand the political socialization process. A model similar to this provides the focus for one of the final chapters of this book.

FIGURE 1.2. A Model To Be Tested

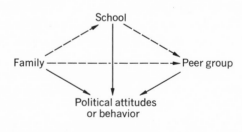

35 Franklin W. Houn, *To Change a Nation* (New York: Free Press, 1961); Robert J. Lifton, *Thought Reform and the Psychology of Totalism* (New York: Norton, 1961); and Stephen and Ethel Dunn, "Directed Cultural Change in the Soviet Union: Some Soviet Studies," *American Anthropologist*, 64 (April, 1962), 328–39.

36 See Chapter 5 for a discussion of this form of re-socialization.

CHAPTER TWO

FAMILY STRUCTURE AND POLITICS

⌘⌘⌘⌘⌘ From the concept of self to his interpretation of sensory impressions, the individual is shaped, within limits of his biological heritage, by his social experiences. The family is the first social group to which he belongs, and the first socializing agency in his life. Mother, father and siblings are the first people with whom he has contact and the first to teach him how to live with others. Such considerations have led many students of personality and human behavior to stress the pivotal role of the family in the general socialization process.

Family and Socialization

Within the family the individual learns his first set of social roles, and in doing so, takes a major step in the process of socialization. He learns what is expected of him as a child and how he should relate to other people. He learns his role within the family power structure, and which family statuses control the resources he needs (food, protection, affection). By imitation and identification he learns, also, what behavior is sex-appropriate in the society and what behavior is not. Within the social setting of the family the individual first forms his self-concepts: the kind of person he perceives himself to be, what assets and liabilities he sees himself possessing, and what he expects of himself in the present and the future.

Thus, the child will carry with him into the school environment a set of role-behaviors and a self-concept that are largely the result of his family training. These may be greatly modified or they may be reinforced by his experiences in the peer group and school. In either case, the attitudes and behavior patterns established in the family will constitute the base for future socialization experiences.

Many students of politics have generalized from the family's broad socialization role to its specific impact upon politics. They consider the unique environment of the family to be the paramount agent of political socialization.[1] Within the family the child has his first experience with authority relationships which he may generalize to larger political systems. Political loyalty, patriotism, national heroes, and devils are all seen as developing early in life.

The view that parents play unique roles in transmitting political culture springs, in part, from the high inter-generational agreement found in party identification and electoral behavior in the United States.[2] Extrapolations from these findings have led credence to the inferences made in other studies as to the importance of parents in *directly* transmitting a wide range of political values and orientations to their children. Recent research, however, has raised important questions concerning the family's role as a total political socializer. Significant incongruities have been found between the political orientations and issue positions held by parents and children within the American family.[3] While party identification and attachments such as national loyalty may be transmitted, the ability of the parents to directly pass on a wider range of political values and issue orientations to their children is less obvious.

If the assumed influence of parents in passing on their political values in a direct one-to-one fashion to their children must be re-assessed, there is little doubt that parents have a profound impact on the formation of certain political orienta-

[1] Herbert Hyman, *Political Socialization* (New York: Free Press, 1959); and James C. Davies, "The Family's Role in Political Socialization," *The Annals*, 361 (September, 1965), 10–19.

[2] See Chapter 3.

[3] Robert D. Hess and Judith V. Torney, *The Development of Political Attitudes In Children* (Chicago: Aldine, 1967), chap. 5; and M. Kent Jennings and Richard G. Niemi, "Family Structure and the Transmission of Political Values from Parents to Child," *The American Political Science Review*, 62 (March, 1968), 169–84.

tions. Moreover, the family has many facets and its political impact can be viewed from less direct perspectives. One such perspective is family structure. Our analysis focuses first on the authority structure in the family and the political relevance of autocratic child reading. The second section, which embodies the major thrust of the structural analysis, examines the conjugal power structure or the relative power of mother and father in the family. Special emphasis is given to the effect of maternal dominance on the political socialization of the children. This section begins with an explanation of the differential effects of mother-only versus nuclear families upon the political development of secondary school adolescents in the Caribbean. The research design allows us to follow the continuing influence of early family socialization in maternal and nuclear families throughout the adolescent's enrollment in secondary school. Finally, we examine an important analog to maternal dominance in the mother-only family: parental power relations in nuclear families in which the mother plays a more dominant role than the father. National data from the United States are used as comparative information.

Autocratic Family and Adolescent Political Deviancy

Considerable literature has been devoted to the influence of authoritarian child-rearing practices upon adolescent attitudes and behavior. Adolescent and child enthnocentrism, guilt, and hostility have all been ascribed to autocratic family environments.[4] Social scientists interested in political behavior have also begun to investigate the relations between strict parental control and political attitudes and rebellion among adolescents.

[4] Sara Lee Dickens and Charles Hobart, "Parental Dominance and Offspring Ethnocentrism," *Journal of Social Psychology*, 49 (May, 1959), 297–303; Alfred L. Baldwin, "Socialization and Parent Child Relationship," *Child Development*, 19 (September, 1948), 127–36; and Robert F. Peck, "Family Patterns Correlated with Adolescent Personality Structure," *Journal of Abnormal and Social Psychology*, 57 (November, 1958), 347–50.

Parental authority appears to be relatively more permissive in the United States than in such countries as Japan and Germany. In their five-nation study Almond and Verba find that American children are more free to participate in family decisions concerning their own activity and to criticize and to speak out about those problems.[5] Consequently family related political rebellion may be less frequent in the United States than in other societies. Moreover, when politics is not a salient factor in the family the rebellion that does occur may be directed against more "visible" objects such as traditional social norms and religious beliefs.[6] Even when the parents are politicized the rebellion may take a restricted political form in which adolescents react only against the most public political identifications of the parents.

Middleton and Putney find that university students' deviations from their perceptions of their parents' liberal-conservative political viewpoint is associated with estrangement between parent and child when the parent is interested in politics. The relationships are not overly strong, suggesting that adolescent rebellion does not play an important role in the formation of these types of political views in American society.[7]

In a comparative study in Belgium, the Netherlands, and France, parental over-protection bred a feeling of political distrust and disaffection among high school and university students. Over-directive parents, who attempt to limit the outside contacts of their children, and who control closely

[5] Erik Erikson, *Childhood and Society* (New York: Norton, 1950); Robert Lane, *Political Ideology* (New York: Free Press, 1962); and Gabriel Almond and Sidney Verba, *The Civic Culture* (Princeton: Princeton University Press, 1963), pp. 346–63.

[6] Elizabeth Douvan and Martin Gold, "American Adolescence: Modal Patterns of Bio-Social Change," in Martin and Lois Hoffman (eds.), *Review of Child Development Research*, Vol. II (New York: Russell Sage Foundation, 1966), pp. 469–528; Robert Lane, "Fathers and Sons: Foundations of Political Belief," *American Sociological Review*, 24 (August, 1959), 502–11.

[7] Russell Middleton and Snell Putney, "Political Expression of Adolescent Rebellion," *American Journal of Sociology*, 68 (March, 1963), 527–35.

their general emotional development inculcate in their children the belief that politicians are not to be trusted, that political parties are useless, and that politics is generally a hostile activity. The relationships are stronger in France and Belgium than in the Netherlands, and may contribute to the negative political attitudes allegedly found among French and Belgian adults. However, even in these latter two countries the parent-student correlations are fairly low.[8]

Among national samples of adults in Great Britain, West Germany, Italy, Mexico, and the United States, those respondents who participated in family decision-making as adolescents are more likely as adults to have a high level of subjective competence, a feeling that the individual can have some influence on governmental decisions. The relationships are strongest among respondents with the lowest education.[9]

Among the political orientations transmitted by the family, party identification stands out as one of the most salient and readily transferred. Because of its visibility it may be one of the more relevant objects of adolescent political rebellion. In the Caribbean study we were able to determine the party identifications of both parents and children, as well as to obtain a measure of the strictness and rigidity of parental control.[10] This measure is based on a number of conceptual considerations and questions.

[8] Frank A. Pinner, "Parental Overprotection and Political Distrust," *The Annals of the American Academy of Political and Social Science,* 361 (September, 1965), 58–70.

[9] Almond and Verba, *The Civic Culture,* pp. 348–49.

[10] Respondents were asked: "In your case has your family been very strict and wanted to have a lot to say about what you did, your friends and the places you went with them, never letting you have your say, or have they been pretty free with you and let you make you own decisions?" The response categories are:
1. Family has always been very strict and never let me have my say.
2. Family has been strict most of the time and hardly ever let me have my say.
3. Sometimes the family has been strict, but sometimes they would let me have my say.
4. Family has been very free with me and I pretty much made my own decisions.
See Appendix A for sample design.

First, is over-strict parental control in the Caribbean culture likely to be manifested among the respondents as deviancy from family party identifications? Second, do we find a rebellion-conformity threshold of family authoritarianism beyond which family dominance discourages rather than encourages political deviancy? Third, is political deviancy higher when politics is a salient issue in the family than when the family is less politicized? Finally, is the authoritarian family environment and the resultant adolescent deviancy likely to be reflected by the offspring in stronger identification with the party preferences of his peers?

TABLE 2.1. *Family Authoritarianism and Students' Party Preference Deviancy from Parents'*

FAMILY AUTHORITARI- ANISM	PARTY PREFERENCE OF STUDENTS		
	Same as Parents (per cent)	Different from Parents (per cent)	N
High 1	83	17	125
2	62	38	230
3	71	29	537
Low 4	82	18	221

Table 2.1 reports the relation of family authoritarianism to political deviancy. First we see a congruity between the party preference of students and parents. However, there is a decrease in respondents' compliance with the party preferences of their parents as family authoritarianism increases—until the most highly authoritarian group is reached. Eighty-two per cent of the students from families where parental dominance is minimized have the same party identification as their parents. With the exception mentioned, compliance decreases as we move from "low" to "high" on the authoritarian family index. This relationship suggests a tendency for secondary students to manifest their rebellion against parental dominance by bolting their parents' political party.

These findings partially reflect those of Maccoby, Mathews, and Morton in their study of young voters in Cambridge, Massachusetts. They report that "it is the children of parents who attempt to exercise strictest control over their children in their teens who most often change away from the political preferences of their parents."[11] They conclude that young voters subjected to strict control by their parents rebel against such treatment by taking different party identifications as an object of their protest.

While political deviancy increases in the Caribbean as parents become more autocratic, the relationship, as noted,

TABLE 2.2. *Family Authoritarianism and Students' Party Preference Deviancy from Parents', within Different Levels of Parental Politicization*

		Same as Family (per cent)	Different from Family (per cent)	N
		PARTY PREFERENCE		
Low Parental Politicization:				
High Parental Authoritarianism	1	89	11	42
	2	54	46	80
	3	59	41	167
Low Parental Authoritarianism	4	71	29	86
Medium-High Parental Politicization:				
High Parental Authoritarianism	1	78	22	76
	2	68	32	150
	3	75	25	361
Low Parental Authoritarianism	4	88	12	135

[11] Eleanor E. Maccoby, Richard Mathews, and Anton Morton, "Youth and Political Change," *Public Opinion Quarterly*, 18 (Spring, 1954), 23–39.

becomes curvilinear in the most authoritarian families. Eighty-three per cent of the children from the most autocratic families have the same party orientations as their parents. This group rivals the students from the least authoritarian families in its compliance with parental party identification. This would seem to indicate a conformity-rebellion threshold of family authoritarianism. Even though the students in group two are raised in authoritarian households, they do not feel the total parental dominance of those in group one—a dominance so oppressive that it discourages rather than encourages political deviancy. Students in the latter group say that their parents are *always* very strict with them and *never* let them have their say.

Where a control for family politicization is imposed, the same pattern and "threshold" emerges (Table 2.2). Among respondents from families of low and medium-high politicization, there is an increase in political deviancy away from the party preference of the parents as family authoritarianism increases. Among the most authoritarian families the relationship again becomes curvilinear, with a sharp increase in adolescent compliance with parental party orientations.

Maccoby and others found that the effect of parental training methods on the political deviancy of young voters was greatest when the parents had a high level of interest in politics. They reasoned that high political interest increased the visibility of party identification as an object of protest.

In Table 2.2, young people from highly authoritarian families (group 1) are among those least likely to deviate from parental preferences, but conformity among this group does decrease by 11 per cent as family politicization increases. This is consistent with Maccoby's finding. However the relationship between autocratic parents, adolescent party deviation, and parental politicization is more complex than this. Higher parental politicization increases political deviancy in the most autocratic families by presumably making party identification a more visible symbol of protest, but it has the opposite effect among more permissive parents (groups 2–4). The average parent-student party identification agreement in groups 2–4 among the most politicized parents is 77 per cent, but it is only 61 per cent among the least politicized parents.

Heightened parental politicization acts as a catalyst in transmitting and maintaining partisan homogeneity in the less autocratic families, while it illuminates party identification as an object of protest in the most authoritarian family.

To determine if rigid parental control is likely to drive adolescents away from the party loyalties of their parents toward those of their peers, an index was designed reflecting students' deviancy from parents toward their peer group. For the purpose of this analysis the index is composed of two broad categories. The first includes all students whose party preference is the same as their parents and peer group. The second includes all respondents whose party preference is the same as their peer group but different from their parents.

Although the row marginals are smaller, the same curvilinear pattern is visible. Students with the strictest parents rival those with the most permissive parents in their adherence to their parents' party identification. This pattern continues when parental politicization is controlled, with similar opposed effects on deviancy at different levels of family authoritarianism.

We can possibly explain the greater adolescent conformity in the Caribbean sample among the most autocratic families in contrast to its deviancy among Maccoby's young Americans by the difference between the two measures of parental control. The American measure has three response alternatives. The most autocratic response is to report that your family "had a lot to say about your friends and the places you went." The question used among Jamaican students is a finer four-point measure in which the most autocratic response ("Family has *always* been very strict and *never* let me have my say") apparently has selected out those families with the most oppressive environment. It is also possible, as we indicated before, that there may be fewer highly autocratic parents in the United States than in other cultures, therefore we would be less likely to find this curvilinear relationship.

Clearly, more detailed study with various measures of family authority patterns and further cross-cultural research is necessary before we can firmly establish the relationship between political saliency and party preference change as a manifestation of protest.

Conjugal Power Structure and the Mother-Only Family

In some of the literature on family socialization, particularly in the national character school, there have been implicit and occasionally explicit allusions to the possible differential effect of parents on the political socialization of their children.[12] Sociologists have expressed interest in the relative power of mother and father in the family circle and the impact of this conjugal relationship upon the socialization of offspring. They reason that variations in family role structure (e.g., maternal *vs.* paternal dominance) have consequences for the internal processes of the family system as well as for the socialization environment it provides.[13] Different parental power structure or gross differences in household composition (e.g., father absence) may provide quite different household personnel with whom the child can interact and identify. Thus different household systems provide different constellations of "significant others" in the early learning process; these varied interaction patterns seem to have differential effects on the socialization of the individual.

Certainly the maternal family, in which the child lives exclusively with his mother, contrasts strikingly with the nuclear household where both father and mother are present. In the first instance, the mother is the controller of virtually all resources desired by the child; in the second, another person is present to mediate and is available as a model for imitation and identification. The "status envy" model of child development would hypothesize that these two types of households have significantly different effects on the socializa-

---

[12] See Robert Lane for a summary of paternal role models from the national character school and a discussion of the effects of paternal rearing practices upon the psychopolitical outlook of the male offspring. Lane, "Fathers and Sons," pp. 502–11.

[13] Murray A. Strauss, "Conjugal Power Structure and Adolescent Personality," *Marriage and Family Living*, 24 (February, 1962), 17–25.

tion of children. The central concept of this model is that the individual's envy of persons who control resources which he himself would like to control leads to covert practice of the envied role, and that through this process the individual begins to identify with the important "other" person and to internalize his (or her) attitudes as well as imitate his behavior.[14]

Thus the physical absence of the father may have greater effect upon male than female children. Father absence could lead to male cross-sex identification. Studies of father-absent families indicate that male children and adolescents tend to show less academic achievement and to be less achievement oriented than individuals in nuclear families.[15] Other studies report that boys from father-absent households develop decidedly effeminate behavior patterns.[16] Males from maternal families are also more infantile, dependent, and submissive than those from households in which the father is present.[17]

[14] Roger V. Burton and John W. Whiting, "The Absent Father and Cross-Sex Identity," *Merrill-Palmer Quarterly*, 7 (April, 1961), 85–95.

[15] John D. Herzog, "Additional Parameters for Educational Planners: Some Thoughts from Research in Barbados," unpublished manuscript, 1964, pp. 12–13; and David McClelland, *The Achieving Society* (Princeton: Van Nostrand, 1961), p. 374.

[16] George R. Bach, "Father-Fantasies and Father-Typing in Father Separated Children," *Child Development*, 17 (March-June, 1946), 63–79; Lois M. Stolz, *Father Relations of War Born Children* (Palo Alto: Stanford University Press, 1954); and Burton and Whiting, "The Absent Father and Cross-Sex Identity."

[17] David Lynn and William Sawrey, "Effects of Father Absence on Norwegian Boys and Girls," *Journal of Abnormal and Social Psychology*, 59 (September, 1959), 258–62; E. Gronseth, "The Impact of Father Absence in Sailor Families upon the Personality Structure and Social Adjustment of Adult Sailor Sons," in N. Anderson (ed.), *Studies of the Family*, Vol. 2, Part I (Gottingen: Vandenhoeck and Ruprecht, 1957), pp. 97–114; P. O. Tiller, "Father Absence and Personality Development of Children in Sailor Families," in N. Anderson (ed.), *Studies of the Family*, Vol. 2, Part II (Gottingen: Vandenhoeck and Ruprecht, 1957), pp. 115–37; and Urie Bronfenbrenner, "Some Familial Antecedents of Responsibility and Leadership in Adolescents," in Luigi Petrullo and Bernard M. Bass (eds.), *Leadership and Interpersonal Behavior* (New York: Holt, Rinehart and Winston, 1961), 237–89. A. F.

These findings have been explained in the following ways. First, male children from mother-child households lack appropriate male figures with whom to interact and identify, and thereby learn sex-appropriate role behavior. As a result, their ego development is retarded as they face debilitating conflicts over their cross-sex identification confounded by the insecurity of being the "sole male provider" in the household. Secondly, mothers in mother-child households are more protective than mothers in nuclear households. They tend to keep their children physically and emotionally dependent upon them longer than do mothers of father-present males. Finally, given the tendency for the parent to be relatively more affectionate and over-solicitous toward the child of the opposite sex, the presence of the father may counteract and check the tendency of the mother to over-protect her son.

The foregoing conceptualization and findings have led us to hypothesize that nuclear and maternal (mother-only) family structures will have differential effects upon the political socialization process. Maternal households will have a greater effect upon male than female respondents in the following ways: (1) males from father-absent families are more likely than females to react to the anxiety of insecure paternal identification with compensatory closed belief systems as measured by the dogmatism scale, (2) the absence of a paternal political stimulant and role model is more likely to retard the political interest of males than females, and (3) maternal dominance will have a more debilitating effect on the feelings of political efficacy among male children than female.

A more concise statement of this model of maternal family socialization is: (1) male respondents from maternal families have more authoritarian attitudes, are less politically interested, and feel less politically efficacious than male respondents from nuclear families, and (2) family structure (nuclear

Henry also reports that males from families where the mother is the chief disciplinarian rank higher on feelings of "self blame" than males from families where the father is the chief disciplinarian. Andrew F. Henry, "Family Role Structure and Self Blame," *Social Forces*, 35 (October, 1956), 34–38.

vs. maternal) has no differential effect upon the authoritarian attitudes, political interest, and sense of political efficacy among female respondents.

Procedure

In the United States, maternal families in which no adult male has resided in the household during child raising are fewer in number and generally restricted to urban slum areas. In less industrialized areas of the world, however, the "World Ethnographic Sample" reports a significantly high incidence of maternal families.[18] In Jamaica, for example, it has been estimated that 25 per cent of the families are maternal.

The Caribbean study conducted in 1964 focused on, among other things, the socialization role of the maternal family. Through a series of indirect and direct questions we were able to differentiate satisfactorily between maternal and nuclear families. During pre-test, an effort was made to validate the family structure responses from the study questionnaire by interviewing a small subsample of families. In no case was there an inconsistency between a reported maternal family and the actual fact.

A maternal family is one in which the child and his (or her) mother have shared a common household while he was growing up, and in which the father or another adult male has not generally been present. This definition does not exclude the possibility that the child's brothers and sisters may have lived in the same household. A nuclear family is one in which the child, his father, and his mother have all shared a common household, exclusive of other adults, when he was growing up.

In addition to information about family characteristics, we also collected data regarding respondent authoritarianism and political efficacy. The scale of authoritarianism is based on the research of Milton Rokeach,[19] who has developed a scale

[18] George E. Murdock, "World Ethnographic Sample," in Frank W. Moore (ed.), *Readings in Cross-Cultural Methodology* (New Haven: Hraf Press, 1961), pp. 193–216.

[19] Milton Rokeach, *The Open and Closed Mind* (New York: Basic Books, 1960).

of general authoritarianism—both left and right—which he calls the Dogmatism Scale.[20] People who score high on this scale are those who have adopted a "closed belief system" as a defense against anxiety. The dogmatic person has a relatively rigid organization of beliefs and expectations. He has an authoritarian outlook on life, and an intolerance toward those who hold opposing beliefs. Dogmatic individuals

> may become disposed to accept or to form closed belief systems of thinking and believing in proportion to the degree to which they are made to feel alone, isolated, and helpless in the world in which they live and thus anxious of what the future holds in store for them.[21]

When we examine the political orientations of these dogmatic or authoritarian types, we find, for example, that those Jamaican students who score high on authoritarianism are most inclined to "agree strongly" with the following statement of explicit political authoritarianism: "What this country needs is a few strong, courageous and tireless leaders in whom the people can put their faith" (Gamma: + .32). When other dependent political variables are examined, a series of weaker but consistent relationships develop which suggest that within the Jamaican political system the authoritarian adolescent has developed a network of beliefs which dispose him toward a strong-man or *caudillo* regime, and away from the processes generally · associated with democratic political systems.

Much literature spanning many different cultures is devoted to the relations between political efficacy and other

[20] Three of Rokeach's dogmatism items were combined into a Guttman-type scale with a CR of 94.3.

The three items are:

1. To work with our political opponents is dangerous because it usually leads to the betrayal of our own side.
2. It is better to be a dead hero than a live coward.
3. When it comes to differences of opinion in religion we must be careful not to give in to those who believe differently from the way we do.

[21] Rokeach, *The Open and Closed Mind,* p. 69.

politically relevant attitudes and behavior.[22] In Jamaica the efficacious student was found to be less ambivalent toward and more supportive of the Jamaican political system and its input and output sub-systems than was his less efficacious counterpart.[23] He was also more likely than his less efficacious peer to participate in latent political and leadership activities in school, to be an interested political spectator, to participate actively in political and election meetings, and to want to engage in politics, part- or full-time, after he graduates.

Results

It was hypothesized that nuclear and maternal family structures will have different effects upon the political socialization process, and that male respondents will be more affected by the environment of the maternal family and the absence of the father than will female respondents. To guard against the possibility that these relationships might be confounded by the class origins of the different family structures, we controlled for social class as well as for sex.[24]

Table 2.3 reports the relation between family structure

[22] Lester W. Milbrath, *Political Participation* (Chicago: Rand McNally, 1965), pp. 56–59; Almond and Verba, *Civic Culture,* p. 247; Angus Campbell *et al.,* "Sense of Political Efficacy and Political Participation" in Heinz Eulau *et al.* (eds.), *Political Behavior* (Glencoe: Free Press, 1959), pp. 170–73; and Angus Campbell, *et al., The American Voter* (New York: Wiley, 1960), pp. 103, 480–81. See also Chapter 6 for further bibliography.

[23] The following four items were combined into a Guttman-type political efficacy scale with a CR of 93.7.

1. When people like me become adults we will not have any influence on what government does.
2. The political views and activities of students are very important.
3. Sometimes politics and government seem so complicated that a person like me can't really understand what is going on.
4. So many other people vote in national elections that it won't matter much to me whether I vote or not when I become an adult.

[24] The social class origin of the respondents' family is determined by an index composed of two items: the occupation and education of the respondent's mother or father—whichever is greater.

TABLE 2.3. *Family Structure and Authoritarianism among Male Students of Different Social Classes*

| | AUTHORITARIANISM | | | |
	Low and Medium (per cent)	High (per cent)	N	Gamma*
Working Class, Males				
Nuclear Family	75	25	83	
Maternal Family	57	43	28	.38
Middle Class, Males				
Nuclear Family	74	26	81	
Maternal Family	53	47	15	.43
Upper Class, Males				
Nuclear Family	71	29	122	
Maternal Family	38	62	13	.60

* Even though the family types included in this table appear to involve nominal categories, the underlying theme stressed is maternal dominance. The assumption is that there is more maternal dominance in maternal than in nuclear families. For this reason it was felt that gamma would provide a more powerful measure of association and would have greater heuristic value than a nominal statistic.

and authoritarian attitudes among male students in different social classes. As hypothesized, male students from maternal families have more authoritarian attitudes than male students from nuclear families. This is true in all social classes. Family structure, however, appears to have comparatively little or no effect upon authoritarianism among females (wc = −.09; mc = −.04; uc = +.20).

A similar pattern is reported in Table 2.4. In both working class and middle class, male students from maternal families are less interested in politics than male students from nuclear families. Only among the more highly politicized upper class does this relationship weaken. Apparently the political culture of the upper class counteracts the inhibiting effect of maternal families. Family structure appears to have little impact upon political interest among females. The correlations between membership in a maternal family and low political interest are: wc = .06, mc = .70, uc = − .13. Be-

TABLE 2.4. *Family Structure and Political Interest among Male Students of Different Social Classes*

| | POLITICAL INTEREST | | | |
	High *(per cent)*	*Low* *(per cent)*	N	*Gamma*
Working Class, Males				
Nuclear Family	40	60	81	
Maternal Family	25	75	28	.32
Middle Class, Males				
Nuclear Family	51	49	81	
Maternal Family	27	73	15	.48
Upper Class, Males				
Nuclear Family	50	50	122	
Maternal Family	54	46	13	−.08

cause of the small number of middle class females in maternal families $(N = 4)$, little or no significance can be attached to the second correlation.

The low political interest among males from father-absent families is not surprising when we see that among those male respondents from nuclear families who see their parents as the most important source of political advice rather than some outside individual or group, over two-thirds (69 per cent) look to their father, rather than to their mother for such advice. Apparently, the absence of the father, an "important other" in the family constellation, removes a powerful political stimulus for the male child.

In the foregoing analysis, a pattern has emerged in which family structure, as predicted, has a differential effect upon the political socialization of male students, while having little effect upon females. Table 2.5 reports the correlation between family structure and political efficacy among male and female students of different classes.

Only among the working class males do we find a correlation between membership in maternal families and low political efficacy. Differing family structures appear to have no significant effect upon the sense of political efficacy among middle and upper class males.

TABLE 2.5. *Gamma Correlation between Maternal Family Structure and Low Political Efficacy among Male and Female Students of Different Social Classes*

	Male	Female
Working Class	.32	.47
Middle Class	.06	.09
Upper Class	.04	.14

Among working class females, those from maternal families feel less efficacious than those from nuclear families. This relationship disappears among the middle class and reappears weakly among the upper class. Like male students, the relation of family structure to a female's sense of political efficacy is primarily a working class phenomenon.

Our cross-sex model of the socialization process in the maternal family did not predict the findings in Table 2.5. Maternal family structure appears to affect the sense of political efficacy among *both* male and female respondents. We cannot explain this effect on females, other than to point out that this is the single female aberration from the model which appears throughout the preceding and following analyses.

To summarize, a predicted pattern develops in which father absence and maternal domination is shown to have an important impact upon the authoritarian attitudes and political interest of male offspring, while it has little effect on females. This is generally true for all social classes on authoritarianism, but only for the lower and middle classes on political interest. Contrary to expectations, there is no sexual differentiation in the influence of family structure upon the development of political efficacy. Maternal dominance affects the sense of political efficacy among both male and female respondents. However, the relationship between family structure and a sense of political efficacy is primarily a working class phenomenon. It seems likely that the greater sense of efficacy found among the more highly educated middle and upper classes counteracts any differential effect mother-only families might have on the socialization of political efficacy.

The high incidence of mother-child families in many of the less industrialized countries of the world suggests the political significance of our findings. However, a more confident appraisal of the effects of mother-only families awaits a broader array of dependent variables. Moreover, the stability of these early learned attitudes during the maturation of the individual is still an open question. This stability provides the crucial link between the family and the political system. For this reason we will now examine the lingering effect of maternal families on the attitudes of their offspring over the secondary school experience.

Stability of Early Learned Attitudes

In Chapter 1 we emphasized that the consistency of early socialized attitudes and behavior, throughout an individual's lifetime, must be treated as a researchable question rather than as a premise. Accordingly the research design in the Caribbean study allows us to inquire into the continuing influence of early family socialization in nuclear and maternal households throughout the student's tenure in the secondary school. Fortunately the dropout rates were sufficiently low so as to have no significant impact upon the assumptions of the quasi-longitudinal design.[25]

In the findings reported in Table 2.6, we will be looking at two things: first, do the differential effects of early family learning persist through the twelfth grade in Jamaican secondary schools? Second, does early family socialization in maternal vs. nuclear families also have a differential effect upon the degree of attitudinal change over the secondary school experience?

[25] Inferences concerning the stability of attitudes and behavior over time are facilitated by the student sample which is based on a set of cross-sections (measurements made at one point in time), and which assumes quasi-longitudinal conditions. That is, students are sampled in the eighth, tenth, and twelfth grades, and assumptions are made about development over time, as though the students in the eighth grade closely resemble the students in the twelfth grade after the passage of four years.

For an extended discussion of the dropout rate see the Appendix A.

TABLE 2.6. *The Lingering Effects of Family Structure: The Relation of Family Structure to Political Attitudes over the Secondary-School Experience*

| | GENERAL AUTHORITARIANISM | | |
	Low and Medium (per cent)	High (per cent)	N
Nuclear Family			
Eighth Grade	75	25	177
Twelfth Grade	81	19	136
Maternal Family			
Eighth Grade	53	47	32
Twelfth Grade	70	30	23

| | POLITICAL INTEREST | | |
	Low (per cent)	High (per cent)	N
Nuclear Family			
Eighth Grade	67	33	177
Twelfth Grade	45	55	136
Maternal Family			
Eighth Grade	72	28	32
Twelfth Grade	61	39	23

| | POLITICAL EFFICACY | | | |
	Low (per cent)	Medium (per cent)	High (per cent)	N
Nuclear Family				
Eighth Grade	36	57	7	177
Twelfth Grade	17	65	18	136
Maternal Family				
Eighth Grade	44	53	3	32
Twelfth Grade	35	61	4	23

Children from maternal families enter the eighth grade with more authoritarian attitudes, less politically interested, and less politically efficacious than their colleagues from nuclear families, and this relationship continues into the twelfth grade. Thirty per cent of the twelfth graders from maternal families have highly authoritarian attitudes, but only 19 per cent of those from nuclear families do. The same pattern of lingering family influence exists with political interest and efficacy. Among twelfth grade students from nuclear families, 55 per cent have a high interest in politics and 18 per cent have a strong sense of political efficacy. On the other hand, only 39 per cent of the respondents from maternal families have a high interest in politics, while less than 4 per cent have a strong sense of political efficacy.

Although students from both maternal and nuclear families appear to increase their political interest and sense of political efficacy as they move from the eighth to the twelfth grade —which suggests, among other things, the socializing influence of the school environment—the greatest increase is among children from nuclear families. The increase in political interest from the eighth to the twelfth grade for this latter group is 22 per cent, compared with only 11 per cent for those from maternal families. Similarly, the decrease in low sense of efficacy from the eighth to the twelfth grade is 19 per cent among children from nuclear families, but only 9 per cent for those from maternal families.

The debilitating effects of maternal family living appear to insulate offspring to some degree from the influences of secondary socialization agencies. However, the decrease in authoritarian attitudes through the secondary school experience was significantly greater for students from maternal families than for those from nuclear families. The student who leaves a particularistic and closed family system and enters the more universalistic and rationalized educational environment of the school may find it more difficult to maintain the simple clichés and close-minded beliefs that characterized his more authoritarian outlook in the family. Yet students from maternal families enter the eighth grade with more authoritarian attitudes than their counterparts from nuclear families, and by the twelfth grade they are still appreciably more authoritarian.

Thus, students from maternal families enter and leave the secondary school feeling less politically interested and efficacious and more authoritarian than those from nuclear families. The early socializing effect of family structure, although diminished, follows the student throughout secondary school, and remains a significant variable in explaining an adolescent's perception of his role in the political system as he approaches adulthood.

Maternal Dominance in the Nuclear Family

Maternal dominance in the nuclear family provides an important analog to the mother-only family situation. Recent research on the effects of conjugal power structure indicates that academic achievement among American boys is lowest in "wife-dominated" homes.[26] Devereux found that American and West German pre-adolescent boys in strongly wife-dominated nuclear[27] families were rated by teachers and peers as more incompetent and dependent than boys from any other type of family.[28]

In a recent national survey of the civic attitudes of elementary school children in the United States, Robert Hess and Judith Torney report relations among nuclear families analogous to those found in mother-only families in the Caribbean. They asked students, "Who is boss in your family?" Elementary school boys in families where the mother is viewed as "boss" have a lower sense of political efficacy and are less interested in politics than those from father-dominant fam-

[26] Glen H. Elder, Jr., *Adolescent Achievement and Mobility Aspirations* (Chapel Hill, N.C.: Institute for Research in Social Science, 1962); See also Lois J. Gill and Bernard Spilka, "Some Non-Intellectual Correlates of Academic Achievement Among Mexican-American Secondary School Students," *Journal of Educational Psychology*, 53 (June, 1962), 144–49.

[27] The term "nuclear" is used in a broad sense in this section. It includes any family in which at least a minimum of both mother and father reside in the home.

[28] Edward C. Devereux, Jr., "Children of Democracy: On the Consequences for Children of Varying Patterns of Family Authority in the United States and West Germany," summary of a paper presented to the Seventh International Seminars on Family Research, Washington, D.C., September, 1962.

ilies.[29] Maternal dominance appears to have no effect on female offspring.

While the political effects of conjugal power structure apparently surface at an early age in the United States, we were able to examine the question directly among a sample of American adults. In Spring 1965, the Survey Research Center interviewed a national probability sample of 1669 high school seniors. In addition to the student reports, interviews were conducted with their parents. The data here are drawn from this parent sample.

Parents were randomly designated so that two-thirds of the mothers and two-thirds of the fathers should have been interviewed. In other words, one-third of the students were assigned father-only interviews, one-third mother-only, and one-third both mother and father.[30] With appropriate weighting we may treat the parents as a probability cross-sectional sample of parents with high school seniors.[31] That this sample departs in some ways from a true adult cross-section need not overly concern us, but it should be noted that the parent cross-section, when compared with a typical adult sample, is more educated and has an age distribution which peaks in the 35–55 range.

In the questionnaire four items seemed suitable for a conjugal power structure index (CPS). Respondents were asked to recall who made decisions and who did the punishing in *their* parents' family. The response alternatives were: father,

[29] Hess and Torney, *The Development of Political Attitudes in Children*, pp. 100, 105.

[30] Because there are more single-parent domiciles headed by mothers and due to the incidence of slightly higher response rates among women than men, the raw number of mother interviews exceeds father interviews, 1106–886. The overall response among parents was 94 percent.

[31] For cross-sectional purposes those parents who constitute a mother-father pair (i.e., where both were designated and both were interviewed) must be given half-weights since only one-half of them would have been selected under the rules employed in the single-parent (family representative) selections. The alternative to half-weighting is subsampling among the parent pairs. The virtue of half-weighting lies in reduced sampling variability. The grand total N for the parents as a cross-section is 1927 (weighted); the number of actual interviews is 1992.

mother, parents acted together, parents acted individually. The third set of questions concerned the parent's relative closeness to his own mother or father: "When you were growing up, how close would you say you were to your father (mother)—very close, pretty close, or not very close." We reasoned that relative closeness might provide some measure of latent influence channels and possible coalitions in the family constellation. The final set of questions concerned the relative education of each grandparent; here, we felt that a family in which mother had more education than father, for example, might provide an indirect measure of maternal dominance.

TABLE 2.7.   *Sex Differences in Respondents' Recall of the Family Environment of Their Parents*

	Male (per cent)	Female (per cent)
Family Decisions		
Father decided	34	24
Mother decided	16	23
Decided together	46	50
Decided individually	4	3
	100	100
Punishment		
Father	27	21
Mother	28	38
Together	30	29
Individually	15	12
	100	100
Relative Closeness		
Closer to father	11	17
Equal	56	49
Closer to mother	33	34
	100	100
Relative Education		
Father more educated	23	25
Equal	48	46
Mother more educated	29	29
	100	100

The four sets of questions were combined into a nine-point index, ranging from paternal dominance through equal dominance to maternal dominance. A father-dominant family would be one in which the father is more educated than the mother, is closer to the children (respondent) than the mother, and generally makes most of the decisions concerning the punishment of the children as well as most of the other decisions in the family.[32]

TABLE 2.8. *Conjugal Power Structure of the Family and Political Efficacy among the Male Offspring at Different Levels of Family Education*

	POLITICAL EFFICACY				
	PRIMARY EDUCATION*				
	Low (per cent)	Medium (per cent)	High (per cent)	N	Gamma**
Mother dominance	60	24	16	42	
Equal dominance	47	31	22	200	
Father dominance	34	43	23	39	.34
	SECONDARY EDUCATION				
Mother dominance	63	23	14	31	
Equal dominance	67	18	15	129	
Father dominance	36	34	30	15	.31
	COLLEGE EDUCATION				
Mother dominance	42	36	21	15	
Equal dominance	58	27	15	52	
Father dominance	51	34	15	18	−.05

* Each education level in this and the following tables should be prefixed: "Some or completed." All row percentages in this and the following tables total 100.
** The rationale for using Gamma in this table is similar to that of Table 2.3.

[32] In the following analysis, CPS index scores from 0–2 will be rated as paternal dominance, 3–5 equal dominance, and 6–8 maternal dominance.

TABLE 2.9. *Conjugal Power Structure of the Family and Political Interest among the Male Offspring at Different Levels of Family Education*

	POLITICAL INTEREST				
	PRIMARY EDUCATION				
	Low (per cent)	Medium (per cent)	High (per cent)	N	Gamma
Mother dominance	16	33	51	42	
Equal dominance	14	23	64	200	
Father dominance	14	20	66	39	.29
	SECONDARY EDUCATION				
Mother dominance	27	13	61	31	
Equal dominance	6	21	73	220	
Father dominance	4	12	84	15	.28
	COLLEGE EDUCATION				
Mother dominance	0	2	98	15	
Equal dominance	10	17	73	52	
Father dominance	19	11	70	18	−.24

Before proceeding further it might be instructive to see how respondents of different sexes view the environment of their parents' family in terms of each of the four items in the CPS index. Of particular interest would be an exaggerated sex bias in the recall of family power structure. While sex differences no larger than those in Table 2.7 were unexpected, one can see that males are more inclined to report that father made decisions than are females (34 per cent *vs.* 24 per cent) and less inclined to report that mother made decisions. Males are also less likely to see mother as making punishment decisions than are females. While males are slightly less inclined than females to report being closer to father, there are no sex differences in reporting closeness to mother. In addition, males and females did not differ significantly in their recall of the relative education of their parents.

TABLE 2.10. *Conjugal Power Structure of the Family and Political Participation among the Male Offspring at Different Levels of Family Education*

	POLITICAL PARTICIPATION			
	PRIMARY EDUCATION			
	None (per cent)	Some (per cent)	N	Gamma
Mother dominance	51	49	49	
Equal dominance	51	49	200	
Father dominance	35	65	39	+.32
	SECONDARY EDUCATION			
Mother dominance	33	67	31	
Equal dominance	38	62	129	
Father dominance	52	48	15	−.31
	COLLEGE EDUCATION			
Mother dominance	32	68	15	
Equal dominance	38	62	52	
Father dominance	48	52	18	−.29

Tables 2.8–10 report the relations between the conjugal power structure of the family and political efficacy, interest, and participation among its male offspring.[33] The relation-

[33] The following four items were combined into an efficacy scale:
1. I don't think public officials care much what people like me think.
2. Voting is the only way that people like me can have any say about how government runs things.
3. People like me don't have any say about what the government does.
4. Sometimes politics and government seem so complicated that a person like me can't really understand what is going on.

Respondents were asked to agree or disagree with each of the items. Questions 1 and 4 are similar to those used in the efficacy index in the Caribbean study.

Political interest is based on the following question: "Some people seem to think about what's going on in government most of the time,

ships are controlled for education level of the family. Maternal dominance correlates with a low sense of efficacy for males whose parents have a primary or secondary level education. However, the relationship weakens and slightly reverses itself among college educated parents.

Political interest (Table 2.9) has a similar pattern. As in the Caribbean, dominance in the United States correlates with low political interest among males from families with primary or secondary education only. But the relationship again reverses itself at the college level. This pattern is repeated in Table 2.10. At the primary school level, maternal dominance retards political participation while father dominance encourages it. At the secondary and college level father dominance discourages participation while mother dominance encourages it.

In view of the reversed effect of family power structure at the higher education levels, one may ask if the maternal role changes with education. Indeed, there is evidence that as one descends the education ladder mothers become increasingly powerful authority figures. Lower class mothers are especially likely to be described as "over-protective, dominating, and demanding."[34] Given the tendency for the parent of the opposite sex to be relatively more protective toward the child, it is in lower class families where boys run the

whether there's an election going on or not. Others aren't interested. Would you say you follow what's going on in government most of the time, some of the time, only now and then, hardly at all."

The political participation index is composed of the following five types of political behavior: attend election meetings, rallies, and so forth, work for one of the parties, belong to a political club or organization, wear a campaign button or use a campaign sticker on the car, and contribute money to a party or candidate to pay campaign expenses.

[34] David Heer, "Dominance and the Working Wife," Social Forces, 36 (May, 1958), 341–47; Elizabeth Wolgast, "Do Husbands or Wives Make the Purchasing Decisions?" The Journal of Marketing, 23 (October, 1958), 151–58; Robert Blood and Donald Wolfe, Husbands and Wives (Glencoe: Free Press, 1960); Rene Konig, "Family and Authority: The German Father in 1955," Sociological Review, 5 (New Series, July, 1957), 107–27; and James C. Rollins, "Two Empirical Tests of a Parsonian Theory of Family Authority Patterns," The Family Life Coordinator (January–April, 1963), 23, "child values" column.

greatest risk of this debilitating experience with their mothers. As the father's relative power increases the mother's tendency to over-protect is checked. But this is more likely to happen in the better educated families. Indeed, Bronfenbrenner found that only among the most educated parents did the father approach or surpass the mother as an influential person in the child's life. This is particularly important for boys, for it was only among college educated parents that the father's predominance over mother in "instrumental companionship" with boys occurred. These were activities involving skill and competition.[35] Thus with a rise in educational level the mother's power is checked, and she tends to be less over-protective.

In the same study, Bronfenbrenner examined the relations between relative parental authority and adolescent responsibility and leadership performance, and comes up with findings that parallel ours: While weak paternal power in nuclear families at lower education levels reduces "responsibility" among male adolescents, a weakening and then a reversal of this trend occurs as we move up in level of education.[36] Maternal authority in the most educated families fosters responsibility in male children, but paternal dominance has a debilitating effect.

Although maternal dominance affects male political interest at all educational levels, it has no significant impact upon the political interest of females. Moreover, the relationships with efficacy and participation among females are also weak and form no discernible pattern.

In short, boys appear to thrive politically in a patriarchal environment—at least in the lower classes—while there is little evidence that the conjugal power structure has a politically relevant impact upon female offspring.

Summary and Conclusion

Maternal dominance appears to play a significant role in the political socialization process. Differences found have not

[35] Bronfenbrenner, "Some Familial Antecedents of Responsibility and Leadership in Adolescents," p. 252.

[36] Bronfenbrenner, *ibid.* pp. 252–56.

always been great, but they have been consistent across cultures in both mother-only and nuclear families.

Students from maternal (mother-child) families in the Caribbean are more authoritarian, less politically interested, and less politically efficacious than respondents from nuclear families. The pattern weakens slightly among the upper classes, but it is only on the efficacy dimension that the differential effect of family structure is exclusively a working class phenomenon. In this case, the more efficacious middle and upper class political culture appears to counteract the differential effects of maternal dominance.

Within the maternal family a predicted cross-sex socialization pattern develops in which the absence of the father and maternal domination increase authoritarian attitudes and decrease political interest among male students, while having little effect on females. On the efficacy dimension, however, no sex differentiation is apparent: Both male and female adolescents from maternal families are significantly less efficacious than their counterparts from nuclear families.

The impact of family experiences upon the political system depends heavily on the ways in which predispositions learned in the family are mediated by the intermediary socialization agencies within society. The stability of these early learned attitudes and behaviors provides the crucial link between family and the political system. When the continuing influence of early socialization in maternal and nuclear families throughout secondary school is traced, we find respondents from maternal families enter the secondary school with a higher level of authoritarianism, feeling less politically interested, and less politically efficacious than their colleagues from nuclear families. More important, this relationship continues through the twelfth grade. Thus the effect of maternal dominance follows the student throughout secondary school and is significant in explaining an adolescent's view of the political process, and his role in it, as he is about to enter adulthood.

An important analog to the mother-only family is the conjugal power structure of the nuclear family in which mother plays a more dominant role than father. Relationships analogous to those found in the Caribbean study were reported in a survey of the civic attitudes of elementary school children in the United States. Elementary school boys from mother-dominant nuclear families had a lower sense of political efficacy and less interest in politics than those from father-dominant families. Maternal dominance appeared to have no effect upon female offspring.

Respondents in a national probability sample of the parents of high school seniors in the United States were asked to recall certain aspects of *their* parents' family environment. A conjugal power structure index was constructed and run against political efficacy, interest, and participation of the respondents. While there are similarities between these findings and those in the Caribbean study, the relationships are more complex.

Male respondents from nuclear families in which the mother is dominant are less politically efficacious, less politically interested, and less likely to engage in political activity than those from father-dominant families. However, this relationship weakens and tends to reverse itself among the most educated families. In other words, at the primary school level maternal dominance has a retarding effect upon political efficacy, interest, and participation. But among the college educated, mother dominance encourages male political involvement.

In all three studies maternal dominance had a debilitating effect upon male offspring—this was particularly true among the least educated families. Generally, conjugal power had little politically relevant impact upon females. Only in the Caribbean did maternal dominance affect female adolescents, and this occurred only on one of three dimensions at the working class level where it lowered their sense of political efficacy.

CHAPTER THREE

MOTHERS VERSUS FATHERS
IN THE FORMATION
OF POLITICAL ORIENTATIONS

Kenneth P. Langton and M. Kent Jennings

▌▌▌▌▌ Now that we have examined the effect of family structure, we turn to the role of parents in directly transmitting political orientations to their children. Parents are usually treated as a unit in the literature and not distinguished according to their individual roles in the political socialization of their children. Moreover, when "parental" characteristics are specified, father attributes are commonly taken as a satisfactory description of the unit. Such assumptions are valid enough for many purposes, but to understand fully the parent-child transmission process within the family circle it is necessary to differentiate the contributions of mothers.

One area in which the family is undoubtedly important is in transmitting party identification. In Jamaica, for example, almost 70 per cent of the students report the same party preference as their parents. Similar agreement was found in Great Britain and Norway. In the United States the distribution and stability of party identifications have had a significant impact upon the political system. Since the 1930's, party preferences have been intimately connected with the "normal vote," which has generally dictated control of national political office.[1] Moreover, the frequency and stability

This chapter is based on a revision and extension by Kenneth P. Langton of an article by M. Kent Jennings and Kenneth P. Langton, "Mothers versus Fathers: The Formation of Political Orientations among Young Americans," *Journal of Politics*, May, 1969.

[1] Angus Campbell *et al., Elections and the Political Order* (New York: Wiley, 1966).

of citizen preferences for either the Republican or Democratic parties has helped to inhibit the rise of new political groupings. This point is underscored when we compare the United States with France. The absence of widespread party loyalties in France has been linked with the historical symptom of French political turbulence—the availability of the unaligned Frenchman for flash party movements. These weak party attachments are associated with certain peculiarities in the French socialization process, including the failure of French parents to communicate their party preferences to their children.[2]

By contrast, most researchers in the United States agree that the political orientation most readily transmitted by parents to their offspring is party identification. Studies of adults and children show, that when the recalled party preference of both parents is the same, up to 80 per cent of the respondents also report that preference.[3] Yet how much each parent contributes to this high congruence is not clear; nor is this question easily resolved, given mother-father agreement. When parental partisanship is mixed or inconsistent the identification of the offspring is more evenly divided between the parties. Little is known about the relative influence of parents on the child's party identification and political orientations in these families. This point provides the grist for our analysis. By examining those instances where mothers and fathers have divergent preferences, the relative influence of each parent in affecting the preferences of offspring can be more readily assessed.

[2] Philip Converse and Georges Dupuex, "Politicization of the Electorate in France and the United States," *Public Opinion Quarterly*, 26 (1962), 23.

[3] Angus Campbell, *et al.*, *The American Voter* (New York: Wiley, 1960), p. 147; V. O. Key, Jr., *Public Opinion and American Democracy* (New York: Knopf, 1961), pp. 295–96; Herbert McClosky and Harold Dahlgren, "Primary Group Influence on Party Loyalty," *American Political Science Review*, 53 (September, 1959), 762; Fred Greenstein, *Children and Politics*, pp. 71–73; and Philip Nogee and Murray Levin, "Some Determinants of Political Attitudes among College Voters," *Public Opinion Quarterly*, 22 (Winter, 1958), 449–63. For a review of the literature see Stephen W. Wasby, "The Impact of the Family on Politics," *The Family Life Coordinator* (January, 1966), 3–23.

The prevailing view on intra-familial interaction in the United States sees the husband-father playing the dominant political role. McClosky and Dahlgren found, for example, that when the inherited political preferences of husbands and wives differ, "there was a tendency for women to switch more often to their husbands' preferences than the reverse."[4] Campbell, Gurin, and Miller observed that "political influence in the marriage relationship seems to go predominantly in one direction," from husbands to wives.[5] The Elmira study also indicates that married women look to their husbands for political information—which they receive.[6] At least one dissenting note has been sounded, although the substantive topic did not involve party preference. March has argued that the traditional division of political labor within the family is changing, and that among the more educated, middle class families there is a greater sharing of political roles.[7]

Notwithstanding this point, the fairly slender soundings of the other inquiries are buttressed by one's intuitive notions and observations about the role of the sexes in American party politics. As with most occupations, men occupy elite positions. More significant, they are more evident at the cadre and mass public levels. Politics is conventionally thought of as sex-appropriate for men, whereas doubts and ambiguities prevail regarding women. In fact, political sex-role differentiation has been detected as early as the fourth grade among American school children.[8] Bearing these tendencies in mind, it is perhaps logical to assume that within the family father will be more likely to influence the offspring's political coloration than will mother.

On the other hand, a small amount of evidence suggests

[4] McClosky and Dahlgren, "Primary Group Influence on Party Loyalty," p. 770.

[5] Angus Campbell, et. al., The Voter Decides (Evanston, Illinois: Row, Peterson, 1954), p. 206; and Robert Lane, Political Life (New York: Free Press, 1959), p. 9.

[6] Bernard Berelson, et. al., Voting (Chicago: University of Chicago Press, 1954), p. 102.

[7] James March, "Husband-Wife Interaction over Political Issues," Public Opinion Quarterly, 17 (Winter, 1953–54), 461–70.

[8] Greenstein, Children and Politics, chap. 6; and Hess and Torney, The Development of Political Attitudes in Children, chap. 8.

that this interpretation of male dominance needs re-evaluation. Two studies of young people based on limited samples and recall data concern the inter-generational transfer of party identification. In one, a group of college students had somewhat greater agreement with their mothers than with their fathers.[9] Another study of young adults in Cambridge, Massachusetts also disclosed greater agreement with mother than father when parents had discrete party preferences.[10]

A potential problem in these and other investigations is that the party preference of the respondent's parents is normally based on the respondent's recall.[11] Such reports may be distorted by a tendency to inflate agreement with parents in order to minimize dissonance, or they may simply be inaccurate. This becomes particularly confounding when one is attempting to determine the relative influence of mothers and fathers who have conflicting party preferences.[12] In this chapter we shall use American data collected directly from mother, father, and child.

Research Design and a Basic Measure

The data comes from the study of political socialization conducted among American high school students. As you will remember, at the core of the study stands a national probability sample of 1669 seniors. One-third of the seniors were randomly designated as cases in which their mothers were interviewed, one-third in which fathers were interviewed, and one-third in which both parents were interviewed. It is this latter group which concerns us.[13]

[9] Nogee and Levin, "Some Determinants of Political Attitudes among College Voters."

[10] Eleanor E. Maccoby, et. al., "Youth and Political Change," pp. 23–29.

[11] For a study comparing the reports of offspring about their parents with the reports of parents themselves see Richard Niemi, "Collecting Information about the Family: A Problem in Survey Methodology," to appear in Frederick Frey and Jack Dennis (eds.), Political Socialization: A Reader in Theory and Research (forthcoming).

[12] Retrospective adult data also fails to take account of what the respondent's identification was at the time he was preparing to leave his family of orientation versus his later identification.

[13] Altogether there were 558 potential student-mother-father triples as a result of this procedure. In practice there are actually 430, or 77

It should be noted that these three categories, while constituting a reasonably representative sample of a population of such triples, do not include the potential cases represented by students who dropped out of school before reaching the twelfth grade—a proportion estimated to be around 26 per cent in the mid-1960's. Thus, the findings are not easily generalized to the universe of triples including this age-grade group. It seems reasonable to suppose, however, that dropouts more often come from broken homes than do twelfth graders, so a goodly number of the remaining potential triples would have left school in any event. Furthermore, the use of social class controls will give some indication of how the remaining triples might have behaved had they been included. Finally, given the strong relation between education and voting turnout, it is probable that the universe actually sampled will be disproportionately represented in the active electorate over time.

Initially we must divide the parental pairs into likeminded versus conflicting combinations. The determination of the homogeneity-heterogeneity of parents' party identification was conditioned by several factors. First, this analysis starts with a set of parental pairs, the great majority of which are homogeneous in party identification, given most reasonable

---

per cent of the potential number. Only one-quarter of the loss comes from outright refusals. The balance is divided between the 51 per cent resulting from non-samples (parent deceased, divorced, or separated) and the 24 per cent due to non-interviews (temporary absence, illness, or other incapacity). Altogether, in 27 per cent of the "lost" cases neither the father nor the mother were interviewed; in 59 per cent the father alone; and in 2 per cent a potential triple was aborted by failure to interview the student. Among actual refusals the rate was moderately higher for fathers than for mothers. Another characteristic of the triples is that there are slightly more boys than girls (54 per cent vs. 46 per cent). This is almost exclusively an artifact of the greater proportion of boys than girls in the original set of potential triads (53 per cent vs. 47 per cent). Finally, even though the raw number of triples is 430, the weighted N is 531. The raw N's were later adjusted to correct for unavoidably imprecise senior class size estimates made when the sampling frame was constructed. Due to missing data (minor party preference, no answer, etc.), the final weighted N for the triples is reduced from 531 to 500.

means of determination. Because the primary target of this study is families involving heterogeneous parental pairs, we did not want to restrict unnecessarily the number of such pairs by insisting that they be bi-polar, that is, a combination of Democrat and Republican. In the analysis the bi-polar pairs as well as other less marked cases of heterogeneity will be examined, either separately or together.

On the other hand, we also felt that triad (mother, father, and child) homogeneity-heterogeneity, in which the designation of parental mix is an important determining factor, should reflect the fact that "undercover partisans," who call themselves Independents, often tend to be partisan in their voting behavior. For example, among those students who first responded that they were Independents, but after an initial probe said they leaned toward the Democrats, 88 per cent later revealed that they would have voted for Johnson in 1964, had they been eligible. Although only 46 per cent of the Independent-Republicans said they would have voted for Goldwater, this must be placed in the context of an election which generated an abnormally high defection rate, about 40 per cent, among marginal Republicans. Comparable figures for the parent sample are 82 per cent for Democratic leaners preferring Johnson and 62 per cent for Republican leaners favoring Goldwater.

Therefore, for most analytical purposes, we treated the parents' seven-point measure of party direction as a three-point scale by ignoring the distinction between strong, weak, and Independent partisans. In other words, a Republican or Democratic parent would be anyone originally identified as (1) strong, (2) weak, or (3) Independent-leaning toward a party. Independents consist of only "pure" types. This means that any parental mix of strong, weak, or Independent-Democrats would make a homogeneous Democratic parental pair. Likewise, any similar mix on the part of both parents and their student offspring would make a homogeneous Democratic triple (Appendix B presents different combinations of parent-student party identifications).

Three major configurations are produced by combining responses to the party identification question from each member of the triad. First are those completely homogeneous triples, wherein the student, mother, and father all share the same general party affiliation. Fifty-seven per cent of the cases fit this description, which belies the popular notion that the family unit is predominantly like-minded. In the second type, mother and father are homogeneous but the student deviates. For example, the parents are Democrats and the offspring is either a Republican or a pure Independent. Seventeen per cent of the triples are of this nature. When this group is divided further it turns out that 59 per cent are homogeneous parents, who have a child attached to the opposite party. Forty-one per cent of this group show a child who is an Independent.[14] In the final pattern the parents are heterogeneous and the offspring agrees with one or, possibly, neither. The father may be Republican, mother Democrat, and the child Republican, i.e., child agrees with father. If the child in this instance was an Independent, he would be classified as agreeing with neither. Out of all triples, 26 per cent fall into this category.[15] Of this sub-total, 54 per cent embrace partisan-Independent parental pairs and 46 per cent involve Democratic-Republican bi-polar combinations.

To summarize, 57 per cent of the triples are broadly homogeneous; 17 per cent have homogeneous parents and a deviating child; and 26 per cent include heterogeneous parents. One immediate conclusion, then, is that the family circle is by no means monolithic in its partisan attachments. This diversity, moreover, is understated since expanding the family constellation to include other children would yield even more complex structures.

To gain some appreciation of the differential pull of mothers and fathers in American families we must first consider briefly the most common parental combinations—those in which parents share the same party identification. Next

[14] This excludes those few cases (N=12) in which both parents are Independents.

[15] Altogether, 72 per cent of the husband-wife pairs are homogeneous, 28 per cent heterogeneous. These figures depart slightly from triple proportions because of missing data. Using the seven-point party identification scale, the tau-b correlation for husband-wife pairs is .59.

is a detailed investigation of the most appropriate parental constellation for our analysis: those families in which mothers and fathers differ in their partisan preferences. Here we scrutinize parent-child agreement in a variety of partisan combinations. Through controls we seek to specify the familial properties which accompany different transmission patterns. Because the patterns found in the area of party identification may extend to other political orientations as well, we also investigate differential parental influence in selected issue areas. In the concluding portion we consider historical changes in the political socialization roles of mothers and fathers. Throughout the analysis the focus will be on the American triads, because of the direct data source. In the final section, however, these findings will be compared briefly with recall data collected from adults in the United States as well as from the student sample in the Caribbean.

Triples with Homogeneous Parental Pairs

One recurrent finding in the electoral behavior literature is that those people who recall that both their parents preferred one of the two major parties generally prefer that party themselves. Our data clearly support these findings: when parents agree, 76 per cent of the students agree with them. However, inter-party differences are present. Among Republican parents, 68 per cent of their offspring prefer that party also (Appendix B). By comparison, among Democratic parents a full 85 per cent of their offspring identify with the Democratic party. Obviously, the Democratic party enjoys greater retaining power among the children of like-minded parents. Moreover, when students do disagree, those from Republican parents are more likely to defect all the way to the opposing party (60 per cent) than are students from Democratic parents (46 per cent). In short, whatever the extra-familial influences acting on today's adolescents, such as Democratic majorities in the nation or the partisan climate of the school community, they are stronger in the direction of the Democratic party than the Republican.

The two subsets of triples with homogeneous parents are of most immediate interest. In the first subset are the students

(76 per cent) who succumb to their parents' identification. The other group (24 per cent) consists of those who fail to follow their parents. First, we shall see if there are any prominent familial attributes which differentiate these defecting students. That is, given like-minded parents, it is conceivable that one parent may be relatively more influential than the other in preventing the deviation of the student. What happens, for example, when the mother is high and the father is low in politicization, when the father is high and the mother low? In order to examine this and similar questions we devised indices of the relative politicization and education of mothers versus fathers.

Given the generally assumed political dominance of the father, it is surprising to learn that he is relatively weak in helping preserve triadic homogeneity. If either parent plays a more impressive role in maintaining the family homogeneity of party preferences, it is the mother. Such a picture emerges from an examination of the relative politicization of the parents as determined by campaign activity.[16] As expected, there

TABLE 3.1. *Relative Campaign Activity Level of Mother and Father and Student Agreement with Party Identification of Homogeneous Parents*

	TRIPLES INVOLVING HOMOGENEOUS PARENTS		
Relative Activity Level of Mother vs. Father	Parents and Student Agree (per cent)	Parents Agree, Student Differs (per cent)	N
Mother higher	85	15	71
Approximately equal	75	25	171
Father higher	73	27	128

[16] Parents were asked if they had performed any of the following activities during any elections over the past ten years: talking to people, going to meetings and rallies, belonging to political clubs, wearing buttons or using stickers, contributing money, and any "other" work. After constructing a six-point index on the basis of the replies, father and mother pairs were then cross-tabulated with three resultant patterns: those where mother had the higher score, those where both were

are more families in which the father shows greater politicization. But when the mother is the more highly politicized, she
has relatively more "pulling power" than the father in maintaining the child's loyalty to his parents' party (Table 3.1). The
net difference is 12 per cent between the case which shows
mother relatively higher than when the opposite prevails. A
similar, though less marked, relationship prevails according to
the parents' relative education. When mother is more highly
educated, triadic homogeneity is more often maintained than
when father is the better educated.

Most assuredly the differences revealed by these measures
are not large in an absolute sense. They must, however, be
placed in the context of conventional notions concerning male
dominance. Not only is that view disputed by this evidence,
but it tends to be replaced by one indicating a slight maternal
superiority within the family circle.

Establishing the different contribution of each parent to
the offspring's partisan attachment when the parents have
identical preferences is a demanding task, and one with which
we are not primarily concerned. Nevertheless, the findings
strongly suggest that the role of mothers in the transfer of
party identification from like-minded parents has been underestimated. Having briefly surveyed and set in place the first
piece of our mosaic with homogeneous parents, we shall now
turn to the more interesting situation in which mother and
father have conflicting party identifications.

Heterogeneous Parents and Inter-generational
Transfer of Party Identification

When parents differ in their party preference, which parent
will seemingly have the greatest influence on the party identification of the offspring? The word "seemingly" is well ad-
vised inasmuch as differential rates of agreement between
students and mothers versus students and fathers will not

---

equal (i.e., on the diagonal), and those where father was higher. This
is the basic procedure followed for all measures used in this chapter
showing the "relative" positions of mothers versus fathers.

prove that one parent is more influential than the other. Such differences provide circumstantial evidence and can, in any event, only point toward patterns calling for explanation.

We noted earlier that heterogeneous parental pairs consist of conflicting combinations among the three positions of Democrat, Republican, and (pure) Independent. For the moment let this requirement be relaxed so the data can be examined under conditions which maximize the number of cases of parental disagreement. The seven-point party identification scale of one parent in each pair is crossed against that of the other parent. The diagonal represents perfect agreement. Every cell off the diagonal shows some measure of disagreement. Among this group of parental "disagreers," the level of mother-student and father-student correspondence provides an initial clue as to differential influence. While the differences are not large, the maternal edge found earlier among homogeneous parental pairs persists. The tau-b correlation between mother and student (.40) is slightly stronger than that for father-student (.35).

Before leaving this broadly defined example of heterogeneity we should consider the possibility that same-sex or cross-sex patterns lie beneath the relationships. For example, fathers may have a particularly strong influence on the party identification of their sons, while having less impact on daughters. This type of relationship would be masked when students are treated as a whole. The tau-b correlations for the four resultant pairs are: mother-daughter = .45, mother-son =.36, father-daughter = .37, and father-son = .34. Clearly, differentiating students by sex does not alter the father-offspring correlations. What slight difference there is suggests, contrary to what might be expected, that daughters are more similar to fathers than are sons. On the other hand, the congruity between mother and daughter is noticeably stronger than is that for any other combination. The overall edge for mother is largely a function of the high mother-daughter symmetry.

Better tests of the parental influence question can be conducted with parents who are more truly heterogeneous in character. As a first step, let us momentarily set aside the bi-polar parents and consider the less extreme case of partisan-Independent families. These comprise 14 per cent of the entire sample, and 54 per cent of all heterogeneous parental pairs. Students in these families are, not surprisingly, more often pure Independents (33 per cent) than are the students as a whole (15 per cent).

These findings add additional evidence that fathers are by no means the decisive positive force in establishing a child's party identification. In the first place, the overall results show 39 per cent of the students agreeing with mother, 37 per cent with father, and 24 per cent with neither.[17] Second, out of all the possibilities for agreeing with the *partisan* parent among these partisan-Independent parent pairs, students agree with the mother 53 per cent of the time, and with the father 47 per cent. Perhaps more significant is the amount of defection to the opposite party. When fathers are partisan, 44 per cent of the students identify with the opposite party, whereas this is true of 24 per cent when mother has the partisan role. If one were trying to demonstrate that mothers more often inspire same-party preference among their offspring, these figures would be comforting, though perhaps not convincing. Since the conventional hypothesis is just the opposite, the modest edge for mothers takes on added weight.

Illuminating as these patterns are, they will be even more persuasive if it can be shown that they hold under each of the four combinations possible in the partisan-Independent mixes: mother Democratic, father Independent; mother Independent, father Democratic; mother Republican, father Independent; and mother Independent, father Republican. One hazard here is that the N's now become perilously low (Table 3.2), so caution must be exercised. In those families with a Democratic-Independent parental mix, a partisan mother has more Democratic pulling power than a partisan father (12 per

[17] From this point onward parent-student correspondence will be reported primarily in terms of percentages rather than rank order statistics. This is due in large part to the fact that the statistics can be disguising internal relationships of special significance for this analysis and to the fact that we wish to examine the fine grain of the agreement patterns.

cent difference) and there are fewer Republican defections (9 per cent difference). Similarly, when the mother is a Republican and father an Independent, she has slightly more partisan pulling power than does a Republican father when mother is an Independent. She also "allows" fewer defections to the Democratic party (22 per cent difference).

TABLE 3.2. *Party Identification of Parents and Offspring among Parents with a Partisan-Independent Party Identification Mix*

PARENTAL PARTY IDENTIFICATION MIX		STUDENT PARTY IDENTIFICATION			
Mother	*Father*	Demo-crat (*per cent*)	Inde-pendent (*per cent*)	Repub-lican (*per cent*)	*N*
Democrat	Independent	51[a]	37	12	20
Independent	Democrat	39	40	21	20
Republican	Independent	21	34	45	14
Independent	Republican	43	17	40	15

[a] Percentages here and in other tables may not appear to be correct given the N's upon which they are based. This is a consequence of rounding off the weighted N's.

The most severe instance of heterogeneous parents is the bi-polar type, that is, one parent is a Republican and the other a Democrat. Altogether, 12 per cent of all the triples include bi-polar parents, and such combinations constitute 46 per cent of all heterogeneous triples. For the children this is potentially the most cross-pressured situation possible. In response, 26 per cent of them adopt a position of independence. Inasmuch as only 10 per cent of students with homogeneous parents are Independents, it must be concluded that the cross-pressures increase the likelihood of an Independent preference. One of the classic solutions to cross-pressures is to adopt an intermediate or neutral position. Temporarily, at least, a sizable fraction of our cross-pressured young adults have elected this course.

Appealing as the classic resolution of cross-pressures may

be, it obviously is not the modal pattern. To the one-fourth who are Independents must be added 40 per cent who identify with the mother's party, compared with 32 per cent sharing the father's. Again the mother, by inference, exerts the stronger pull on the party loyalties of offspring.[18] What is significant is not that the net difference between the pull of mothers compared with fathers is only 8 per cent, but that there is *any* difference at all in this direction.

TABLE 3.3. *Party Identifications of Bi-Polar Parents and Their Offspring*

PARENTAL PARTISAN IDENTIFICATION MIX		STUDENT PARTY IDENTIFICATION			
Mother	*Father*	Democrat (per cent)	Independent (per cent)	Republican (per cent)	N
Democrat	Republican	44	21	35	37
Republican	Democrat	29	38	33	23

The next question is whether mothers hold this edge in each of the two subsets of bi-polar parents. That is, does a Democratic mother with a Republican husband exert the same pull as a Republican mother with a Democratic husband? Table 3.3 presents the relation between the party preference of bi-polar parents and their offspring with partisan direction clearly shown. In bi-polar pairs consisting of a Democratic mother and a Republican father the proportion of Democratic offspring is greater (15 per cent difference) than for those pairs in which the father is Democratic and the mother Republican. This is accomplished primarily by the reduction in the number of student Independents in those bi-polar families with a Democratic mother. When mother is Republican and father Democrat, both the father's influence and that of the Democratic majority culture are partly coun-

[18] Taking the partisan-Independent and bi-polar varieties together, 40 per cent of the students side with mother, 35 per cent with father, and 25 per cent with neither.

teracted, while the ranks of the Independents are swelled. The classic middle-ground solution to the cross-pressure dilemma occurs more frequently where the mother's identification is contrary to national trends. It is as though the student, unable to jump completely to the trend-consistent preference of his father, edges away only so far as to become Independent.

Our analysis demonstrates that students fail to gravitate in disproportionate numbers to their fathers' party. Indeed, there is a modest counter-movement, a pattern which tends to hold regardless of particular identification mixes. Such findings suggest that traditional assumptions about male political dominance in the American family may need to be revised.

Factors Associated with Differential Parental Influence

Although we cannot say precisely why students agree more with mothers than with fathers, it is possible to identify some properties accompanying such differences. We noted that parent-student sex combinations had some bearing on intergenerational agreement when heterogeneity was broadly defined. Mother-daughter symmetry was higher, while son's agreement was generally distributed more evenly between the two parents. A similar pattern occurs for the more tightly defined heterogeneous families, that is, the combination of both bi-polar and partisan-Independent parents. Nevertheless, there is some tendency for same-sex agreement among both boys and girls (Table 3.4, panel 1).

Dividing these triples even more finely underscores the strength of the mother-daughter agreement. Among partisan-Independent families, 47 per cent of the daughters agree with mothers, 29 per cent with fathers, and 24 per cent with neither. In the bi-polar case the picture is nearly identical: 48 per cent agree with mothers, 31 per cent with fathers, and 21 per cent with neither. For boys this same-sex pattern is not as persistent. Although boys more often follow father than mother in partisan-Independent families—33 per cent mother, 44 per cent father, 23 per cent neither—they go with one parent as readily as with the other in bi-polar families—33 per cent mother, 33 per cent father, 34 per cent neither. Each parent may receive some advantage from same-sex imitation, but mother is clearly the chief beneficiary.

TABLE 3.4. *Party Identification of Parents and Offspring among Parents with Heterogeneous Identifications, by Five Characteristics*[a]

| CHARACTERISTIC | STUDENT'S PARTY IDENTIFICATION SAME AS: | | | |
	Mother (per cent)	*Neither (per cent)*	*Father (per cent)*	*N*
1. Student Sex				
Girls	47	22	30	56
Boys	33	28	39	73
2. Relative Closeness to Parent				
Closer to Mother	51	19	30	48
Equally close to each	26	30	43	69
3. Mother-Father Education Level[b]				
Some college or more	42	28	30	50
High school completed	41	24	35	53
Less than high school	31	23	46	26
4. Campaign Activity Level of Mother versus Father				
Mother higher	59	13	28	23
Equal	41	22	38	55
Father higher	30	34	36	52
5. Partisanship Level of Mother versus Father				
Mother higher	56	15	29	41
Equal	40	31	29	35
Father higher	26	30	43	53

[a] Due to the small N's involved, the partisan-Independent and bi-polar parental pairs are combined to form a larger single group of heterogeneous parents.
[b] This measure is derived by taking the highest education reported by either parent. The tau-b correlation between the education of mother and father is .55.

One explanation for the mother's surprisingly competitive position in drawing agreement from the child may lie in the natural reservoir of affective ties between mother and child. On the average, children feel closer to their mothers than to their fathers. This is certainly true of twelfth graders. Among all students with heterogeneous parents 56 per cent felt equally close to both, 39 per cent felt closer to their mothers, and only 5 per cent felt closer to their fathers than to their mothers. This pattern is stronger among girls than boys, but even for the latter, the ratio is lopsided. If the child perceives a parental division of opinion, it seems probable he will side with the parent to whom he feels closest, simply because he associates favorable objects or opinions with that parent. Even if the child does not perceive conflict, the cue-taking mechanism would still seem to be such that cues from the more favorably viewed parent would be received and internalized more frequently.

Because of the dearth (and probably very unusual circumstances) of cases in which the child feels closer to his father than to his mother, our analysis will be restricted to two situations: (1) affect toward each parent is equal, and (2) the mother is viewed more warmly. The data suggest that mothers do indeed benefit from the greater emotional attachment (Table 3.4, panel 2). When the student feels equally close to each parent, he is less compelled to make a choice or to be drawn toward the mother, and the traditional pattern of male superiority prevails. Even in this instance of equally close attachments, however, the father's absolute pull is not as high as the mother's when she is perceived more warmly. The point is that the closer relationship with mother helps reduce typing father as the appropriate model for political identification.

Other characteristics, such as education, may also condition the relative influence of each parent. Even though the findings are mixed, it is commonly held that the middle class is characterized by greater role sharing.[19] By extension, one

[19] Urie Bronfenbrenner, "Socialization and Social Class Through Time and Space," in E. E. Maccoby, *et al.*, *Readings in Social Psychology* (New York: Holt, Rinehart and Winston, 1958), pp. 400–24; Urie Bronfenbrenner, "Some Familial Antecedents of Responsibility and

might expect the mother to be relatively more influential in families with higher education. This is not to say that mothers are less dominant among the working class, but that the relative nature or style of their authority changes with social class. Indeed, the form of maternal dominance in lower class families may actually hinder the mother-child transmission of party identification (see Chapter 2).

A control for parental education has a moderate effect on the correspondence between the party preference of heterogeneous parents and their offspring (Table 3.4, panel 3). Children with the least educated parents more often agree with their fathers. But beyond that level, conformity with the mother increases. Overall, the mother-father differences move steadily from a 15 per cent deficit for mother in the less educated families to a 12 per cent advantage in the college educated ones. Breaking out the bi-polar cases exaggerates this movement: the net differences run from a 15 per cent deficit for mother in the lowest category to a 26 per cent advantage among college-level parents. Since parent-student correspondence is affected by educational status, and since our sample underrepresents low-education families, it seems probable that mother-student agreement among our sample is somewhat higher than it would be for a sample reflecting all triples involving this age group.

Aside from the realignment of parental roles by education, this variable is also related to female political activity. March, among others, argues that the ethos of sexual political equality has been more readily absorbed by the better educated, resulting in more political specialization between husbands and wives and a general upsurge in female activity.[20] From voting behavior research it is well-known that participation differences between men and women decrease as education rises.

When we examined homogeneous parental pairs in which

Leadership in Adolescents," pp. 239–71; David Miller and Guy Swanson, *The Changing American Parent* (New York: Wiley, 1958); Russell Lynes, *A Surfeit of Honey* (New York: Harper, 1957), pp. 49–64; and William Ogburn and Meyer Nimkoff, *Technology and the Changing Family* (Boston: Houghton-Mifflin, 1955), chap. 1.

[20] March, "Husband-Wife Interaction over Political Issues."

the mother was more politicized, the student was most likely to agree with his parents. A similar process seems to be at work among heterogeneous parents, a process which redounds to the benefit of mothers. After mothers and fathers are categorized according to their relative campaign activity, and this in turn is crossed against parent-student agreement, a clear tendency emerges for the student to follow the more politicized parent (Table 3.4, panel 4). This pattern is particularly striking, however, when mother is the more active parent; there is 23 per cent more agreement with her than with father when he is most active. Significantly, the greatest incidence of student independence occurs in those families in which father is most active, and where there is likely to be severe cross pressure between affective ties to mother and the attraction of a more highly politicized father.

Another indicator of politicization—perhaps less subject to education influences—appears in parental responses to the party identification items. In addition to determining the party affiliation of the respondent, these questions also reveal the intensity of attachment among the partisans. The bi-polar parental pairs can thus be divided into those in which higher intensity is characteristic of the mother, the father, or they share the same intensity. Pairs involving an Independent-partisan combination are more difficult to handle since the intensity of "Independents" is not ascertained. However, one may assume that the Independents are less intensely partisan. Hence the analogue for the more intense parent in the bi-polar case will be the partisan among the Independent-partisan pairs. For convenience we combine the results from these two types of heterogeneity, but it should be emphasized that our conclusions hold for both types.

Just as relative campaign activity level affects the rate of parent-student agreement, and particularly agreement between mother and student, so also does relative intensity. Panel 5 of Table 3.4 shows conclusively that the child is more likely to agree with the parent who is the more intense (or partisan). Although this holds no matter whether that parent is the mother or the father, the mother is still the greater beneficiary. The net mother-father difference is

27 per cent when mother is the more intense, compared with 17 per cent when father is. Again, there is an increase in the disagreement with both parents once we leave the triples in which the mother is the more politicized.

Even though similar processes are apparently at work in heightening student agreement with a particular parent, these processes affect mother-student agreement more sharply than father-student rates. This is most noticeable for the politicization measures. A comparison of the top and bottom rows of Panels 4 and 5 in Table 3.4 indicates that mother-student agreement is much more sensitive to the relative levels of parental politicization. What seems to happen is that when her activity and intensity levels increase, the mother becomes a much more visible and salient source of political information. She reaps corresponding benefits as her relative position improves. This is only partially true for fathers, mainly because the child more often adopts a position independent of both mother and father as the latter becomes more politicized. As the mother's politicization level becomes relatively high, traditional habits of sex-typing are attenuated. She is seen as having political views in her own right and presumably tests and exercises them in the family circle. Should the secular forces at work in society result in an even greater proliferation of politically dominant wives, one would expect maternal strength in the transmission process to increase.

A more complex interpretation is possible: Those mothers who take a greater part in political life also have other characteristics which help attract the loyalty of their children. That is, women who are more politicized than their husbands may also be the kind of mothers who fight for—and often win—the allegiance of the children when husband and wife differ. Maternal personality differences may account for some of this disparity. A parental pair in which the mother has the stronger ego may heighten her pulling power with the children. To test this hypothesis we devised a relative ego-strength index.[21] When relative ego strength was crosstabulated with parent-child party agreement there was little

[21] Responses to three items formed an ego or opinion strength scale with a CR of .94. Mothers and fathers were then compared within each pair to determine their placement on the scale.

evidence that a relatively stronger ego worked to the advantage of either the mother or the father.

However, ego strength may work in a more indirect way. Does the incidence of homogeneous, partisan-Independent, and bi-polar parental pairs, for example, reflect the ego strengths of the respective parents? It may take a wife with a strong ego to maintain her party preference in the face of her husband's disagreement. On the other hand, the distance between the political preferences of husband and wife in homogeneous pairs is only a matter of intensity, and in the partisan-Independent pairs the gap would again be smaller than in the bi-polar type. In neither case does a wife need as strong an ego to maintain her partisan identity, or so we hypothesized.

That mothers in bi-polar families hold a relatively higher ego position than their husbands is in fact the case. Among both homogeneous and partisan-Independent pairs, the father has the higher ego 42 per cent of the time, and among bi-polar pairs this is true 29 per cent of the time. Mothers in bi-polar situations have more ego parity with their spouses. If parental ego strength affects the determination and maintenance of particular husband-wife partisan constellations, then once these family types have been established, other familial properties, such as affective relations between parents and children, may guide the actual transmission process.

In assessing the vitality of each of the five independent variables which had an observable impact on parent-student agreement, it is important to know if the relationships shown in Table 3.4 persist under certain control conditions and if they are cumulative. Unfortunately, the subsample size interferes with extensive use of multi-variate controls. What we have settled for is a series of contingency tables in which the initial bivariate relationships of Table 3.4 have been controlled by each of the other independent variables, one at a time. Moreover, because we have emphasized conditions maximizing mother-student accord—and since this accord is more responsive to change in the independent variable categories than is father-student similarity—we will focus on agreement with mother.

We first must determine the degree to which the original student-mother agreement at the bivariate level persists under controlled conditions. One approximate way to assess the importance of the independent variable is to count the number of times, out of all the controlled possibilities, that the original bivariate relationship for mother-student congruence is maintained. The number of possible comparisons equals the sum of the categories within the control variables—ten or eleven depending on the variable being controlled.[22]

Only one characteristic emerges completely unscathed if this criterion is used. Regardless of the controls used, students who feel closer to their mothers always agree more often with her than do students who feel equally close to both parents. The difference in mother-student agreement ranges from 49 per cent when the control is mother being more active in a campaign, down to 12 per cent in those families in which at least one parent has completed high school.

Although the range of agreement by student sex is one of the smaller initial ones, the basic pattern is persistent. The absolute level of agreement with mother changes within categories of the control variables, but girls continue to side with their mothers more than boys do. Out of all possible comparisons, in only one case is this pattern reversed, and in that instance the margin is narrow.

The next most frequent instance in which original patterns persist is relative partisanship level and relative campaign level. In each case, there are three deviations from the original configurations. These occur almost exclusively in cells involving the middle points of the two indexes, that is, where mother and father are equal in partisanship and in campaign activity. The "noise" in the relationships thus takes place when other factors might be expected to exert random and idiosyncratic effects.

Least impressive of the predictor variables, when other factors are controlled, is parental education. The original

[22] When controls are being exercised on the two-category independent variables (sex and relative closeness) the number of comparisons is eleven; when the variables have three categories (parental education, relative activity level, and relative partisanship), the number is ten.

bivariate pattern was not particularly strong, student-father agreement showed a more orderly relationship to educational status than did mother-student agreement. The basic pattern for the latter is repeated in only four of the control categories; nor is the result appreciably different when father-student accord is considered since the pattern persists in but five of the possibilities. Despite these inconsistencies, parental education does affect the relationships, particularly at the extremes. In addition, our sample excludes dropouts, who come disproportionately from lower educated families. Including these families might well have strengthened the relation of education to agreement patterns.

To say that at least four of the five explanatory characteristics continue to have an effect on mother-student (and usually father-student) agreement when each of the other variables is controlled is not to say that cumulative effects are not operative also. On the contrary, a persuasive case can be made that variations in mother-student symmetry are well described by additivity principles, as some examples will illustrate.

We noted previously that relative closeness to mother as

TABLE 3.5. *Party Identification of Mother and Offspring among Parents with Heterogeneous Identifications, under Two Sets of Control Conditions*

RELATIVE CLOSENESS TO PARENT	PARTISANSHIP LEVEL OF MOTHER VS. FATHER					
	Mother Higher (*per cent*)		Equal (*per cent*)		Father Higher (*per cent*)	
Closer to mother	64[a]	(17)	50	(14)	40	(17)
Equally close to each	34	(23)	31	(21)	16	(25)

STUDENT SEX	CAMPAIGN ACTIVITY LEVEL OF MOTHER VS. FATHER					
	Mother Higher (*per cent*)		Equal (*per cent*)		Father Higher (*per cent*)	
Girls	70	(8)	50	(24)	38	(24)
Boys	53	(15)	33	(31)	23	(28)

[a] Cell entries show the percentage agreeing with the mother out of the total N for that cell, that is, the number within the parentheses.

well as the mother's relative level of partisanship were positively related to adopting the mother's party identification. When the variables are combined, as in the top half of Table 3.5, they produce a rather extraordinary range. Thus, when the child feels closer to mother and mother is the more partisan parent (upper left cell), nearly two-thirds of the students agree with her. At the other extreme, when the child feels equally close to each parent and father is the more partisan (lower right cell), agreement with mother is reduced to about one-sixth. Clearly, each of the two characteristics has some impact, but the combined effects are even more impressive.

Another example combines student sex and the relative campaign efforts of mothers and fathers. Both variables continue to exhibit "independent" effects within each level of the other, but the cumulative pattern is striking. In fact, assuming the independent variables are uncorrelated, the value for each cell comes extremely close to the expected value dictated by the additivity model.[23] As a practical matter, the results mean that girls in families where mothers are the politicos are about three and one-half times more likely to acquire their mother's preference than are boys in homes where the father is the more politically active.

These progressions are not atypical of the results obtained when any two of the conditioning factors are observed simultaneously. No variable emerges that seems strong enough to resist completely the strength of any other characteristic. At the same time, the addition of another characteristic tends to operate in a systematic, additive fashion. Given the small N's involved, one must be cautious in making conclusive statements. It is also apparent that we have not been able to express in precise statistical terms the independent and cumulative processes involved in producing mother-student

[23] As it turns out, these two variables are absolutely uncorrelated. Indeed out of the ten pairs formed from the five independent variables eight are uncorrelated while the other two have modest tau-b coefficients of .14 and .21. Working with the grand mean, row means, and column means the predicted values for each cell in the two panels of Table 3.5 were calculated. The size of the errors ranged from 0 to 3 in the second panel with an average of 1.5. In the first panel the additive process is somewhat less strong; the range of errors is 0 to 11, with an average of 4.

identity in heterogeneous triples. Nevertheless, the findings point decidedly toward the set of circumstances that are likely to maximize such identity.

Other Value Orientations

Aside from basic consensual orientations to the political community, party identification stands out as the political disposition most readily passed from generation to generation. At least this seems true according to current appreciation of political learning. It seems worthwhile to see if the tendencies uncovered regarding party preference patterns among the triads can be generalized to other value orientations. In doing this, we run some risk of introducing random and time-specific responses, since most value orientations (as usually tapped) lack the stability associated with party identification.[24] On the other hand, it seems likely that these will be no greater for fathers than for mothers, and no greater for boys than for girls, although such manifestations may be greater for students than for parents.

Our basic finding regarding party identification is that students with heterogeneous parents do not more often agree with their fathers; in fact, there is a persistent tendency for higher congruity with their mothers and less defection to the opposite party. Similar tests can be made with issue-orientations. Five issue-questions, producing dichotomous answers, will be employed. To these will be added political cynicism scale scores, divided into low, medium, and high categories. The dichotomous issues produce combinations analogous to bi-polar pairs on party identification, such as:

	Mother pro Father con	Mother con Father pro
Student pro		
Student con		

[24] A classic demonstration is by Philip E. Converse, "The Nature of Belief Systems in Mass Publics," in David Apter (ed.), *Ideology and Discontent* (New York: Free Press, 1964), pp. 206–61.

If the agreement patterns (excluding cynicism) are analyzed in terms of this four-fold table, the tau-b correlations run from .03 to .23, thereby indicating greater mother-student congruence in every instance. These correlations are obviously modest, but they are perfectly suitable for rejecting the father-dominant model of value transmission.

It is also instructive to present the results in terms of percentage distributions. Without exception there is higher agreement with mother than with father (Table 3.6, total column). Two of these differences are so slight as to be virtual ties. Yet even they are significant for rejecting the hypothesis of greater cue-taking from fathers. It seems the greater incidence of student-mother alignment is not confined to the vital area of party preference.

Dividing the students according to sex preserves, with only one exception for each sex, the general direction of the findings. Girls are a shade more likely to agree with their fathers over the federal government's role in integrating the schools, whereas boys more often side with their fathers on the question of allowing prayers in public schools. Without larger samples to work with, it is difficult to account for these deviations from the more common pattern.

These relationships do not take into account the direction of the parent and student responses. The consistent edge of mothers over fathers could result from high student-mother agreement when mother responds one way and father the opposite (e.g., mother pro, father con), but not for the reverse situation (mother con, father pro). In practice there are some sizeable differences in the N's and percentage distributions for those two bi-polar combinations. If there were a national adult majority position on each of the five issues, it could conceivably affect basic parent-student agreement patterns, particularly if the mother typically sided with the majority culture.

Before testing this proposition we first examined the frequency distributions on each of the five issues as determined by the responses of homogeneous parents. The majority position was clearly revealed in each instance, the lowest ratio being the 3:1 level found on the "communist taking office"

TABLE 3.6. *Heterogeneous Parents and Students on Six Issues, by Sex of Parent and Student*

ISSUE	GIRLS		BOYS		TOTAL	
	Agree with mother (per cent)	Agree with father (per cent) N	Agree with mother (per cent)	Agree with father (per cent) N	Agree with mother (per cent)	Agree with father (per cent) N
U.S. participation in United Nations	80	20[a] (15)	53	47 (35)	61	39 (50)
Allowing Communist to take office	61	39 (78)	53	47 (90)	57	43 (168)
Political cynicism	56	44 (127)	58	42 (139)	57	43 (266)
Federal role in integrating schools	47	53 (59)	61	39 (67)	54	46 (126)
Allowing prayers in public schools	64	36 (34)	42	58 (48)	51	49 (82)
Allowing public speeches against religion	52	48 (62)	51	49 (89)	51	49 (151)

[a] Percentages add to 100 going across each subdivision.

issue. As with party identification, so with these five issues: when both parents adopt the majority position their offspring are more likely to agree with them. When homogeneous parents adopt a minority viewpoint at odds with national inclinations, their children are more likely to be in disagreement. Thus inter-generational value transmission within the family is heightened when those values are consonant with those of the larger political culture.

More pertinent to our original inquiry, when parents' opinions differ, the mother draws an agreement edge from her offspring regardless of her issue position. When she takes the majority position on an issue she draws more student agreement than does father when he takes the same position. Conversely, she also gains more agreement in the minority position than does father when he is in the minority.

Historical Perspectives

Given the age and class composition of our sample, we should be cautious about extending these findings to more diverse populations. However, data from at least one American national cross-sectional sample support this picture. The source is the Survey Research Center's 1964 national election study. Recall information was obtained about the party identification of the respondent's parents during his childhood. For a variety of reasons, the proportion of heterogeneous parents is lower than in the student-parent study (11 per cent versus 26 per cent). Combining both partisan-Independent (N = 36) and bi-polar families (N = 84), it turns out that 47 per cent of the respondents agreed with their mother's (recalled) preference, 38 per cent with their father's, and 15 per cent with neither.[25]

[25] These figures actually exceed those for the triples in suggesting the greater influence of mothers. Straightforward comparisons are not easily made, however, because (1) more students are currently Independent than is true of the adults (2) adults less often fail to agree with either parent (3) the students may later change their preferences (4) the adult data on their parents are based on recall and (5) while the adult sample represents the population of adults over 21, the high school senior sample—as noted previously—excludes the dropout portion

Most striking are the reports from adults who recall that their parents had bi-polar preferences. Table 3.7 shows that respondents from such environments more often wind up agreeing with their mothers.[26] This pattern is most obvious in the case of Democratic mother-Republican father pairs. In view of partisan trends since the New Deal, one might argue that the greater adoption of mother's identification is an artifact of historical currents. If this is true, it should hold for the opposite case of Democratic father-Republican mother pairs. Clearly, it does not. Not only do these fathers share less in the historical bonus, but they are actually out-paced by their Republican wives, who receive more offspring "loyalty" than their Democratic husbands.

Working with the triples, it was determined that the

TABLE 3.7. *Bi-Polar Parental Party Identifications and Adult Offspring Party Identification in a National Adult Sample* (*SRC 1964 Election Study*)

OFFSPRING PARTY IDENTIFICATION	PARENTAL PARTISAN IDENTIFICATION MIX	
	Mother Democrat Father Republican (*per cent*)	Mother Republican Father Democrat (*per cent*)
Democrat	69	44
Independent	0	6
Republican	31	50
	100	100
	(32)	(52)

of the population. It should also be noted that the pattern reflected in the text is true of the bi-polar parents situation—which constitutes 70 per cent of all heterogeneous cases—but not true of the partisan-Independent types, where fathers have a slight edge over mothers among boys.

[26] This is a finding initially presented in John S. Appel and Bert A. Rockman, "Political Socialization: Stability and Change of Intergenerational Effects over the Life as They Affect Partisan Identification," unpublished M.A. thesis, University of Michigan, 1966, particularly pp. 16–46.

mother's influence varied by educational level. The adult election sample reveals a similar picture. Respondents with a grade school education agree slightly more often with their fathers. Beyond that level mothers outpull fathers by about 15 per cent at all educational levels.[27] Subjective identification with the working or middle class provides another basis for differential effects. Thus working class people (N = 67) agree with their fathers as often as with their mothers—43 per cent each, with 15 per cent agreeing with neither. Comparable figures for middle class respondents (N = 50) are 30 per cent fathers, 54 per cent mothers, and 16 per cent neither. Fathers' preferences, then, are more likely to be manifested among lower class and less well-educated children.

The maternal edge reflected in both American samples is also found among Caribbean students. Those respondents (N = 170) who reported that their parents supported different parties (bi-polar) generally agreed with their mother (43 per cent) more than with their father (38 per cent)—19 per cent agreed with neither. Like their North American counterparts, mothers' advantage increased slightly as parental education increased. But unlike the less educated fathers in the United States, the lowest status fathers in Jamaica were also slightly outdistanced by their wives in securing party agreement from their offspring (4 per cent difference).

While the heritage of slavery allegedly relegated males to a social status equal to or lower than that of females in the Caribbean, contemporary historical changes seem more predictive of our findings in the Caribbean, as well as of changing familial influence patterns in other less industrialized countries. For illustrative purposes we shall focus on an explanation of those historical processes as they seemed to have affected conventional assumptions regarding male dominance of political matters in the nuclear family in the United States. At least two factors are involved.

First, during the period preceding female suffrage, ap-

[27] Unfortunately the education of the respondents' parents was not obtained in the 1964 study.

parently husbands and fathers provided the most political cues in the family. It seems highly unlikely that wives and mothers exercised as much influence during this period, since they were without the stimulus of electoral participation. Any change as a result of extending the franchise would work to the advantage of a net increase in mother's influence. We observed, for example, that when mother was the more politicized parent she did exceptionally well in drawing offspring agreement.

A second historical factor, possibly more generally applicable, is increased education attainment in twentieth-century America. As noted earlier, differences in political participation between men and women diminish the higher their educational level. More education has apparently given women a greater sense of socio-political equality. Again, any change as a result of more education would redound to the mother's advantage regarding political cue-giving and modeling in the family. Much the same argument could be made concerning the expansion of the middle class.

If this line of thinking is correct, it should be observable in the 1964 American adult sample. (Ideally we should have a sample from an earlier point in time which would reflect more of the pre-female suffrage period.) Younger respondents should show more deviation from father's identification and greater attraction toward mother's. Dividing the respondents into three age categories (18–34, 35–54, and 55 and older) reveals that the absolute level of agreement with father falls off noticeably the younger the age grouping. Concomitantly, there is a rise in the proportions agreeing with neither parent. One way of expressing these age shifts is to note mother's net advantage over father. This figure is 22 per cent among the youngest age group ($N = 33$), but only 4 per cent among the middle age ($N = 49$), and 6 per cent among the oldest ($N = 37$). Rather than a manifestation of life-cycle effects, it would seem that these differences are historical and generational.

Once the forces of female political participation and rising education were set in motion, they were abetted by certain structural properties of the family in increasing the relative importance of the mother. That is, early affective ties and emotional dependences between child and mother could now be expected to have some carryover into political matters, especially for children who happened to have parents with dissimilar preferences. When parental conflict is present —whether the offspring recognizes it or not—the resolution is likely to favor the parent for whom affect is highest and expressive ties closest. Such choice-making can occur during the pre-adult years or during early adulthood when there is greater opportunity to exercise political preferences. Historically, then, a multiple effect occurred as legal and sociological-educational changes began to interact with the psychological properties of the nuclear family. The traditional view of differential parental influence fails to take account of these dynamics.

CHAPTER FOUR

FORMAL ENVIRONMENT:
THE SCHOOL

Kenneth P. Langton and M. Kent Jennings

‖‖‖‖‖ As the individual matures and begins to explore beyond the family environment, he confronts other groups and institutions which also socialize him to politics. Many of these experiences take place within the context of the school. Such secondary agencies often support the attitudes and behavior patterns established in the family environment, but they can also foster new political orientations.

Schools can inculcate political beliefs formally through conscious, planned instruction, as well as informally through inadvertent, casual experiences in the school milieu. They have been deemed so important in this general process that Hess and Torney state categorically: "The public school is the most important and effective instrument of political socialization in the United States."[1] However, the relative importance and the extent of the school's impact is still an unsettled question. This is particularly so among adolescents. At the secondary school level very little has been done to examine systematically the selected aspects of the school environment. To gain some insight into the role of the school's formal environment we will explore, in this chapter, one of its most prominent features: the effect of the civics curriculum upon

---

This chapter is based on a revision by Kenneth P. Langton of an article by Kenneth P. Langton and M. Kent Jennings, "Political Socialization and the High School Civics Curriculum," *The American Political Science Review,* September, 1968.

[1] Hess and Torney, *The Development of Political Attitudes in Children,* p. 101.

the political attitudes and behavior of American high school students.

Many studies, including Gabriel Almond and Sidney Verba's five-nation survey, stress the crucial role played by formal education in the political socialization process:

> [None of the other variables] compares with the educational variable in the extent to which it seems to determine political attitudes. The uneducated man or the man with limited education is a different political actor from the man who has achieved a high level of education.[2]

There has, however, been much controversy over the objectives and impact of civic education. While most educators agree that the development of good citizenship is important, the "good citizen" is something of an ideal type whose attitudes and behavior vary with the values of those defining the construct. Still, when the literature on the development of civics is examined, a few consistent themes appear. The civics course should increase the student's knowledge about political institutions and processes, make him a more interested and loyal citizen, and increase his understanding of his own rights and the civil rights of others. Good citizenship, moreover, does not exist *in vacuo;* it demands active political participation as well as loyalty and interest.[3]

In addition to curriculum itself, school climate, peer groups, and teachers may contribute to the political socialization process within the schools, but the contribution of each is unclear.[4] Since the influence of the informal school and peer group is examined in Chapter 5, it seems worthwhile, now, to

[2] Gabriel Almond and Sidney Verba, *The Civic Culture,* pp. 135–36.

[3] See, for example, Educational Politics Commission, *Learning the Ways of Democracy: A Case Book in Civic Education* (Washington: National Education Association of the United States, 1940), chap. 1; and Henry W. Holmes, "The Civic Education Project of Cambridge," *Phi Delta Kappan,* 33 (December, 1951), 168–71.

[4] For related bibliography and a general discussion see James S. Coleman, "Introduction" in James S. Coleman (ed.), *Education and Political Development* (Princeton: Princeton University Press, 1965), pp. 18–25.

review briefly the role of the teacher before turning to a discussion of curriculum effects.

Although there have been few systematic studies of overt teacher impact on students' political values in natural classroom settings, the political beliefs of the classroom teacher certainly have an important potential for reinforcing or undercutting the stated objectives of the formal program of civic education. Evidence suggests that public school teachers are often hostile or uncommitted to democratic principles. In a study, only 43 per cent of the secondary school teachers responded that police *should not* have the power to censor movies and books in their cities. Other responses indicate a pattern of uncertainty or rejection concerning the Bill of Rights.[5] However, as a direct transmitter of political values, the classroom teacher may be in a relatively weak position. Many teachers avoid "controversial" political subjects in the schoolroom while opting for "safer" but presumedly less stimulating topics.[6] When we examined American high school students' perceptions of the quality of their civics teachers to see if teacher performance affected the political impact of their civics curriculum, we found that controlling for teacher performance did not significantly alter curriculum effect.[7] Perhaps the most significant adults in the high school socialization system are those who control role assignments which are important *within the adolescent culture*, for example, the athletic coach or the drivers' education teacher.[8]

Turning to the curriculum, it is apparent that attempts to

[5] John Weiser and James Hayes, "Democratic Attitudes of Teachers and Prospective Teachers," *Phi Delta Kappan*, 47 (May 1966), 470–81.

[6] Harmon Zeigler, *The Political World of the High School Teacher* (Eugene: University of Oregon, the Center for the Advanced Study of Educational Administration, 1966).

[7] See pp. 98–99.

[8] Albert D. Ullman, "Sociology and Character Education," in Franklin Patterson, *et al.* (eds.), *The Adolescent Citizen* (Glencoe: Free Press, 1960), pp. 206–23. For experimental evidence on the dubious role of the college teacher as an agency of change see Everett K. Wilson, "The Entering Student: Attributes and Agents of Change," in Theodore M. Newcomb and Everett K. Wilson (eds.), *College Peer Groups* (Chicago: Aldine, 1966), pp. 84–87.

assess its actual impact have produced controversial conclusions. College studies, which examine general curriculum effects (for example, liberal arts *vs.* natural science programs) upon the political values and beliefs of students have generated inconsistent results.[9] Because of the lack of comparative research designs and controls for pre-selection, as well as the differences in the institutional cultures examined, the impact of college curricula is still an open question.[10]

Other inquiries have had more focus. Arthur Kornhauser and Albert Somit, among others, used student panel studies to measure attitude changes resulting from exposure to one or more specific courses. Kornhauser found significant changes in attitudes toward liberal economic positions among students in an economics class. However, Somit concluded that introductory courses in political science which emphasized personal political participation had no significant impact on the students' own attitudes along that dimension.[11]

[9] C. Robert Pace, "What Kind of Citizens Do College Graduates Become," *Journal of General Education*, 3 (April, 1949), 197–202; W. H. Holtzman, "Attitudes of College Men Toward Non-Segregation in Texas Schools," *Public Opinion Quarterly*, 20 (1956), 559–69; Theodore Newcomb, *Personality and Social Change* (New York: Dryden, 1943); Rose Goldsen, *et al.*, *What College Students Think* (Princeton: Van Nostrand, 1960); A. J. Drucker and H. H. Remmers, "Citizenship Attitudes of Graduated Seniors at Purdue University," *Journal of Educational Psychology*, 42 (1951), 231–35; Irvin J. Lehman, "Changes in Attitudes and Values Associated with College Attendance," *Journal of Educational Psychology*, 57 (April, 1966), 89–98; and Walter P. Plant, "Longitudinal Changes in Intolerance and Authoritarianism for Subjects Differing in Amounts of College Education Over Four Years," *Genetic Psychology Monographs*, 72 (1965), 247–87.

[10] Allen H. Barton, *Studying the Effects of College Education* (New Haven: Edward Hazen Foundation, 1959), p. 76; Charles G. McClintock and Henry A. Turner, "The Impact of College upon Political Knowledge, Participation and Values," *Human Relations*, 15 (May, 1962), 163–76; and Theodore M. Newcomb, "The General Nature of Peer Group Influence," in Newcomb and Wilson (eds.), *College Peer Groups*, p. 2.

[11] Arthur Kornhauser, "Changes in the Information and Attitudes of Students in an Economics Class," *Journal of Educational Research*, 22 (1930), 288–308; Albert Somit, *et al.*, "The Effect of the Introductory Political Science Course on Student Attitudes Toward Political

At the high school level, research on the association between curriculum and political socialization has also been mixed. In a quasi-experimental study of three high schools in the Boston area, Edgar Litt found that civics courses had little impact upon students' attitudes toward political participation, but that these courses did affect students' "political chauvinism" and "support of the democratic creed."[12] Experimental pedagogical methods have also resulted in some observable short-term cognitive and affective changes.[13] However, other studies of the relations between social studies courses and politically relevant attitudes report either inconclusive or negative results. The early New York Regents' Inquiry on Citizenship Education, which found that the quantity of work done in social studies was not reflected in changed "citizenship" attitudes, was reinforced by the Syracuse and Kansas studies of citizenship[14] and data from the Purdue Opinion Panel.[15]

Participation," *American Political Science Review,* 52 (December, 1958), 1129–32; and Marvin Shick and Albert Somit, "The Failure to Teach Political Activity," *The American Behavioral Scientist,* 6 (January, 1963), 5–8. Also see James A. Robinson, *et al.,* "Teaching with Inter-Nation Simulation and Case Studies," *American Political Science Review,* 60 (March, 1966), 53–65; and Charles Garrison, "The Introductory Political Science Course as an Agent of Political Socialization" (Unpublished Dissertation, University of Oregon, 1966).

[12] Edgar Litt, "Civic Education Norms and Political Indoctrination," *American Sociological Review,* 28 (February, 1963), 69–75.

[13] See, for example, C. Benjamin Cox and Jack E. Cousins, "Teaching Social Studies in Secondary Schools and Colleges," in Byron Massialas and Frederick R. Smith (eds.), *New Challenges in the Social Studies* (Belmont, California: Wadsworth, 1965), chap. 4; and Robert E. Mainer, "Attitude Change in Intergroup Programs," in H. H. Remmers (ed.), *Anti-Democratic Attitudes in American Schools* (Evanston: Northwestern University Press, 1963), pp. 122–54.

[14] Franklin Patterson, *et al., Adolescent Citizen,* pp. 71–73; Roy A. Price, "Citizenship Studies in Syracuse," *Phi Delta Kappan,* 33 (December, 1951), 179–81; and Earl E. Edgar, "Kansas Study of Education for Citizenship," *Phi Delta Kappan,* 33 (December, 1951), 175–78.

[15] H. H. Remmers and D. H. Radler, *The American Teenager* (New York: Bobbs-Merrill, 1962), p. 195; and Roy Horton, Jr., "American Freedom and the Values of Youth," in H. H. Remmers (ed.), *Anti-Democratic Attitudes in American Schools,* pp. 18–60.

Almond and Verba asked adult respondents to recall if time had been spent teaching politics and government in their schools. They compared the level of subjective political competence of individuals who replied affirmatively with those who reported negatively. The data show "a relatively clear connection between manifest political teaching and political competence in the United States, Great Britain, and Mexico."[16] They conclude that manifest teaching about politics can apparently increase an individual's sense of political competence, but this is less likely to happen in nations such as Germany and Italy where educational systems have been dominated for most of the respondents' lifetime by anti-democratic philosophies.

In addition to such mixed findings, there is also some question as to the potential of the secondary school for political socialization. By the time students reach high school many of their political orientations may have crystallized or have reached a temporary plateau. Recent research[17] on the political socialization of American children indicates that the elementary school years are critical in forming basic political orientations.[18] Perhaps, too, high school civics courses offer little that is new to students; they may provide only another layer of essentially redundant information.

Granting either or both of these points, one should perhaps not expect dramatic movements simply on the basis of one or two courses. However, some incremental changes should be visible. One might also expect differential incremental effects according to some central characteristics of the students, their

[16] Almond and Verba, *The Civic Culture,* p. 361.

[17] Robert D. Hess and David Easton, "The Role of the Elementary School in Political Socialization," *The School Review,* 70 (1962), 257–65; David Easton and Robert Hess, "The Child's Political World," *Midwest Journal of Political Science,* 6 (August, 1962), 229–46; Robert Hess and Judith Torney, *The Development of Political Attitudes in Children;* Greenstein, *Children and Politics.*

[18] On the other hand, Adelson and O'Neil find important political cognitive development taking place during the adolescent years. See Joseph Adelson and Robert O'Neil, "The Growth of Political Ideas in Adolescence: The Sense of Community," *Journal of Personality and Social Psychology,* 4 (September, 1966), 295–306.

families, the school, the curriculum, or the political orientations themselves. We now turn to an examination of such
possibilities.

Study Design

The data are from the national survey of American high
school seniors conducted by the Survey Research Center of
the University of Michigan in 1965. As noted, interviews
were held with a national probability sample of 1669 high
school seniors, distributed among 97 secondary schools (public
and non-public). An important feature of the sample is that
it was drawn from a universe of twelfth graders; school dropouts in that age category are therefore automatically elimin-
ated. For all but 6 per cent of the sample, each student's
mother or father, designated randomly, was interviewed.
Finally, in order to determine some general academic and
structural characteristics of each school, interviews and questionnaires were given to school officials.

The social studies courses taken by each student were
determined in the following way: In each school a list was
made of courses offered during grades ten through twelve.
Each course offered in a school was read to the respondent
and he indicated if and when he had taken it during the
past three years—that is during the tenth, eleventh, or twelfth
grades.

We were particularly interested in those courses commonly
referred to as high school government or civics courses. These
ranged from the usual American Government and Problems
of Democracy courses, through Political Science, Americanism,
Communism and Democracy, to International Relations, World
Citizenship, and Comparative Politics. Contemporary History
courses, which were essentially studies of current events, were
also included. Normally, however, we distinguished between
history courses on the one hand, and civics courses on the
other. While both types of courses (as well as other social
studies) may have an impact on students' political orientations,
we shall generally limit our focus to the civics curriculum.

Each student was scored according to the number of
government courses he had taken during his three years of

high school. About one-third of the students had taken no civics courses at all, and of those who had, the great majority had taken no more than one (Table 4.1). Therefore, in the following analysis when we talk about the direct impact of the civics curriculum upon political orientations, it will mean for most students the difference between no civics and one civics course. Since a civics course is usually taken as a requirement, we may assume that there is little self-selection.[19]

TABLE 4.1. *Number and Type of Civics Courses Taken by American High School Seniors in Grades 10–12*

Number of Courses	Per cent	Type of Course Among Those Taking A Course	Per cent
0	32	American Government	67
1	59	American Problems	37
2+	9	Other	10
	100		114[a]
	N = (2060)[b]		N = (1401)

[a] Percentages exceed 100 because some students have taken more than one course.

[b] This is a weighted N resulting from a factor applied to correct for unavoidably imprecise estimates made at the time the sampling frame was constructed. All results reported here are based on weighted N's. In the case of multivariate analysis using data from the parents as well as students, the base weighted N will be 1927 because interviews were not held with 6 per cent of the students' parents.

Table 4.1 also shows a breakdown of the *type* of course taken. The division is between the more frequently offered American Government course, the less popular American Problems course, and a sprinkling of more esoteric types. The "Problems" course is commonly called Problems of Democracy, Contemporary Problems, Problems of American Life, and so forth. Schools typically offer either American Government or

[19] A regional pattern is present. Appreciably more students in the West and Midwest had taken such courses than was true in the South or, especially, in the Northeast. It appears that this variation did not influence our findings. Other personal and school characteristics did not discriminate among takers and non-takers of civics courses.

American Problems, although they are occasionally found together, and infrequently—in non-public or especially small schools—neither course may be offered.[20] Whereas American Government courses focus sharply on the forms, structures, backgrounds, and traditions of American political life, the Problems courses are more eclectic; they emphasize a wider scope of socio-political activities, are more contemporary in nature, and are typically organized around problems of American public life. Because of the different emphasis and formats of the two types of courses, educators have suggested that they will have differential effects.

In selecting the dependent variables for this analysis, we attempted to touch on many of the consistent themes in the civics literature which are germane for political science. Rather than examine only one or two variables, we have included a wide variety so that the possible variations in effects may be uncovered.

1. *Political knowledge and sophistication.* For better or worse, performance on factual examinations is the main way success of course and teacher is evaluated. Students were asked six questions about contemporary political events and personalities. The pattern of response formed a Guttman-type political-knowledge scale.[21] Another measure (explained below), touching more directly on political sophistication, ascertained the students' perception of ideological differences between political parties.

2. *Political interest.* A hallmark of those who think political education important in the United States is that it en-

[20] For a more detailed account of social studies curriculum offerings see M. Kent Jennings, "Correlates of the Social Studies Curriculum: Grades 10–12," in Benjamin Cox and Byron Massialas (eds.), *Social Studies in the United States* (New York: Harcourt, Brace & World, 1967).

[21] Respondents were asked to identify (1) the number of years a U.S. Senator serves (2) the country Marshall Tito leads (3) the number of members on the U.S. Supreme Court (4) the name of the governor of their state (5) the nation that during World War II "had a great many concentration camps for Jews," and (6) whether President Franklin Roosevelt was a Republican or a Democrat.

The six items formed a Guttman scale with a coefficient of reproducibility (CR) of .92.

courage citizens to take an active interest in political affairs. Although numerous studies of adults suggest that the schools and other socializing agencies fall short of the goals envisioned by the authors of civics textbooks, it is nevertheless possible that these achievements would be even less impressive in the absence of such courses. Among the many measures of interest that were available, we have relied on the answers to a straightforward inquiry.[22]

3. *Spectator politicization.* A more direct measure of interest in political matters is how much students consume political content in the mass media. If the civics curriculum spurs an interest in politics, this should be reflected in greater media consumption. Separate soundings were taken of students' behavior regarding television, newspapers, and magazines.[23]

4. *Political discourse.* Even more dramatic evidence of the success of the civics experience would be an increase in the adolescent's conversations about public affairs or politics. There are relatively few ways the high school senior can (or does) assume an active role in politics, so the frequency of political conversations is not an improbable surrogate for forms of adult-level political activity. For present purposes, the student's report of the frequency in which he discusses politics with his peers will be used.[24]

5. *Political efficacy.* The belief that one can affect political outcomes is a vital element in predicting political behavior. Easton and Dennis found a rising sense of efficacy as the child progresses through elementary school.[25] Much of civic

[22] "Some people seem to think about what's going on in government and public affairs most of the time, whether there's an election going on or not. Others aren't that interested. Would you say you follow what's going on in government and public affairs most of the time, some of the time, only now and then, or hardly at all."

[23] Students were asked how often they "read about public affairs and politics" in newspapers or magazines and how often they watched "any programs about public affairs, politics, and the news on television."

[24] "Do you talk about public affairs and politics with your friends outside of classes?" (If yes) "How often would you say that is?"

[25] David Easton and Jack Dennis, "The Child's Acquisition of Regime Norms: Political Efficacy," *American Political Science Review,* 61 (March, 1967), 25–38; Almond and Verba, *The Civic Culture,*

education's thrust is toward developing a sense of political competence. Efficacy was measured by the students' responses to two items.[26]

6. *Political cynicism.* While trying to create interest in politics and a sense of efficacy, the civics curriculum almost inevitably tries to discourage feelings of mistrust and cynicism toward the government. Indeed, cynicism seems in part to be antithetical to a feeling of civic competence.[27] A six-item scale was used to differentiate the students on this dimension.[28]

7. *Civic tolerance.* Considerable discussion exists in the citizenship literature about the necessity for inculcating norms of civic tolerance. Even though the curriculum materials and the teachers often fail to grapple with the complexities of

---

chap. 12; and Angus Campbell, *et al., The American Voter* (New York: Wiley, 1960), pp. 103–05, 480–81.

[26] The following two items were used to construct a three-point political efficacy scale with a CR of .94.

1. Sometimes politics and government seem so complicated that a person like me can't really understand what's going on.
2. Voting is the only way that people like my mother and father can have any say about how the government runs things.

[27] Robert E. Agger, Marshall Goldstein, and Stanley Pearl, "Political Cynicism: Measurement and Meaning" *The Journal of Politics,* 23 (August, 1961), 477–506.

[28] The following six items formed a political cynicism scale that had a CR of .92.

1. Over the years, how much attention do you feel the government pays to what the people think when it decides what to do?
2. Do you think that quite a few of the people running the government are a little crooked, not very many are, or do you think hardly any of them are?
3. Do you think that people in government waste a lot of money we pay in taxes, waste some of it, or don't waste very much of it?
4. How much of the time do you think you can trust the government in Washington to do what is right?
5. Do you feel that almost all of the people running the government are smart people who usually know what they are doing, or do you think that quite a few of them don't seem to know what they are doing?
6. Would you say the government is pretty much run by a few big interests looking out for themselves or that it is run for the benefit of all the people?

these norms, a proper and necessary role of civics courses is seen as creating support for the Bill of Rights, due process of law, freedom of speech, recognition of legitimate diversity, and so forth.[29] In order to probe the effect of civics courses on such beliefs, a three-item civic-tolerance scale was devised.[30]

8. *Participative orientation.* Instilling a propensity toward participation in public life becomes especially evident as a civic education goal as the adolescent approaches legal age. In particular, one might hypothesize that this ethic would displace a more basic orientation formed at an early age, such as loyalty to country. Responses to an open-ended question tapping students' views of the "good citizen" form the basis of the participative-orientation measure.[31]

Before turning to the findings, it may be instructive to consider some of the factors which could affect the relations between exposure to civics and the dependent variables. For example, one could argue that a positive association between exposure and political knowledge will be found only among students from less educated and less politicized families. This "sponge" theory maintains that children from more culturally deprived families are less likely to be saturated with political knowledge and interest in the family environment, therefore they are more likely to be affected by the civics curriculum when they enter high school. Conversely, one might hypothesize that the child from the more highly educated family is most likely to have developed the minimal learning skills and sensitivity to politics which would allow him to respond to civics instruction.

[29] See Byron Massialas, "Teaching American Government in High School," in Cox and Massialas, *Social Studies in the United States,* pp. 167–95.

[30] The following three agree-disagree questions formed a Guttman scale with a CR of .94.
1. If a person wanted to make a speech in this community against religion, he should be allowed to speak.
2. If a communist were legally elected to some public office around here, the people should allow him to take office.
3. The American system of government is one that all nations should have.

[31] The question wording is found on page 109.

The academic quality of the high school is also germane. A school which sends 75 per cent of its seniors on to a four-year college might be presumed to have a significantly different and better academic program than a school which sends only 15 per cent of its students.

Since we are focusing on civics courses rather than on history courses—taken in moderate to heavy amounts by virtually all high school students—we want to be sure that we are measuring the independent effect of the civics curriculum and not the interactive effect of the history courses. One can easily think of other possible predictor variables: grade average, sex, political interest, and so forth.

The problem of multiple predictors clearly calls for some form of multivariate analysis. We chose the Multiple Classification Analysis Program (MCA).[32] This examines the relationship of each of several predictors to a dependent variable at a zero-order level, and while the other predictors are held constant. Eta coefficients and partial beta coefficients indicate the magnitudes of the relationships for zero-order and partial correlations, respectively. The program assumes additive effects and combines some features of both multiple regression and analysis of variance techniques. Unlike conventional regression procedures, it allows predictor variables in the form of nominal as well as higher order scales, and it does not require or assume linearity of regression.

In the subsequent analysis, seven variables were held constant while the independent effect of the civics curriculum was examined. The seven variables are (1) quality of the school,[33] (2) grade average, (3) sex, (4) student's political interest,[34] (5) number of history courses taken, (6) parental education, and (7) parental politicization (discussion of pol-

[32] Frank Andrews, James Morgan, and John Sonquist, *Multiple Classification Analysis* (Ann Arbor, Michigan: Institute for Social Research, University of Michigan, 1967).

[33] School academic quality is based on the per cent of seniors going on to four-year colleges or universities in each school. This information was obtained from school sources.

[34] When political interest was examined as a dependent variable in the MCA analysis it was, of course, dropped as a control variable.

itics within the family). Information about the last two variables was based on interviews held with the students' parents, not from students' reports, as is commonly the case.

Findings for the Whole Sample

One of our first findings is that scant differences emerge in the dependent variables as a consequence of whether the student had taken a more traditional American Government course or the more topical, wider ranging American Problems course. There is a consistent, though quite small, tendency for students taking the former course to consume more political content in newspapers, magazines, and on television, and to discuss politics with peers more frequently. But compared with students taking the American Problems course, they more often stress the loyalty (48 per cent *vs.* 37 per cent) rather than the participation aspect of good citizenship. Aside from these rather meager differences, students taking the two major types of courses are virtually indistinguishable in terms of their political orientations. Knowing this, we may proceed with some confidence to treat both types of course-takers (and those taking a sprinkling of other courses) together, and to focus our analysis primarily on the amount of exposure: none, one, or two courses during grades ten through twelve.

The results offer strikingly little support for the impact of the curriculum. It is true that the direction of the findings generally agrees with the predictions already advanced. That is, the more civics courses the student has had, the more likely he is to be knowledgeable, to be interested in politics, to expose himself to the political content of the mass media, to have more political discourse, to feel more efficacious, to espouse a participative (versus loyalty) orientation, and to show more civic tolerance. The possible exception is the curvilinear relation between course-taking and political cynicism. Thus the claims made for the importance of civic education courses in high school are vindicated, if one considers only the direction of the results.

However, it is perfectly obvious from the size of the correlations that relationships are extremely weak, in most in-

stances bordering on the trivial. The highest positive eta coefficient is .06, and the highest partial beta is only .11 (for
political knowledge).[35] Our earlier speculation that course-
taking among older adolescents might result in only incremental changes is borne out—with a vengeance. Indeed, such
small increments raise serious questions about the usefulness
of government courses in senior high school, at least as these
courses are at present. Furthermore, the impact of the history
curriculum under the same control conditions is as low or
lower than the civics curriculum.[36]

It could be argued that the inclusion of a key variable, for
example, the quality and type of teaching, would produce
different effects among those students who have taken one or
more courses. This may be true. However, given the meager
zero-order correlations, it is doubtful if that impact would be
particularly large. As mentioned earlier, we examined the
students' perceptions of the quality of their civics teachers to
see if this affected the impact of the civics curriculum and we
found that teacher performance did not significantly alter curriculum effect.[37] Another factor which might elicit differential

[35] For convenience, partial beta coefficients will be referred to as
betas or beta coefficients. The beta coefficient is directly analogous to the
eta, but is based on the adjusted rather than the raw mean. It provides
a measure of the ability of the predictor to explain variation in the
dependent variable after adjusting for the effects of all other predictors.
This is not in terms of per cent of variance explained. The term beta is
used because "the measure is analogous to the standardized regression
coefficient, i.e., the regression coefficient multiplied by the standard
deviation of the predictor and divided by the standard deviation of the
dependent variable, so that the result is a measure of the number of
standard deviation units the dependent variable moves when the explanatory variable changes by one standard deviation." Andrews, *et al.*,
Multiple Classification Analysis, p. 22.

As mentioned earlier, the MCA program assumes additive effects.
While some interaction may be present, a close scrutiny of the statistical
analysis makes it doubtful if the impact is particularly large.

[36] In a preliminary analysis the impact of taking social studies
courses as a whole was also examined. The number of social studies
courses taken accounted for little difference in the students' orientations.

[37] We were interested in what effect the students' perceptions of the
quality of their civics teachers and courses, as well as the sex of the
teacher, might have on the relationships. Students were asked to rank

patterns among students is the content of the materials used and the nature of classroom discussion. This contingency, however, not only faces, in large part, the same difficulty as does the teacher role, it also confronts the reality of considerable uniformity in curriculum materials and the domination of the market by a few leading textbooks.[38]

Do these findings mean that the political orientations of pre-adults are highly resistant to change during senior high school years? This possibility cannot be easily dismissed. Certainly the pre-high schooler has already undergone, especially in the American context, several years of intensive formal and informal political socialization. He may have developed, by the time he reaches secondary school, a resistance to further formal socialization at this stage in his life cycle. But there is an alternative explanation. If the course work is largely redundant, there is little reason to expect even modest alterations. By redundancy we mean not only repetition of previous instruction—though there is surely a surfeit of that—but the duplication of cues from other information sources, particularly the mass media, formal organizations, and peer groups. Students who do not take civics courses are probably exposed to these other sources in approximately the same doses as those who are enrolled. Assuming that this is the case, and that the courses provide relatively few new inputs, one consequence would be lack of differentiation between course takers and non-course takers.

For these reasons it would be well to look at courses and

---

each of the courses they had taken from extremely good to extremely poor. They also ranked the quality of their teachers in the same way. Prior to the MCA analysis the relations between the civics curriculum and the dependent variables was examined within contingency tables controlled for course and teacher ratings. Course and teacher ratings had no consistent, significant effect upon the relationships. Controls for sex of the student's teacher also produced no significant differences.

[38] See James P. Shaver, "Reflective Thinking, Values, and Social Studies Textbooks," *School Review*, 73 (1965), 226–57; Frederick R. Smith and John J. Patrick, "Civics: Relating Social Study to Social Reality," and Byron Massialas, "Teaching American Government in High School," both in Cox and Massialas (eds.), *Social Studies in the United States*, pp. 105–27, 167–95.

teachers which avoid redundancy and examine the finer grain of teacher performance and course content. Another strategy, and one we will adopt here, would be to look at sub-populations of pre-adults where redundancy might be less frequent than for adolescents in general. Among the universe of possible sub-populations, perhaps none is as distinctive as the Negro minority. The unique situation of Negroes in American social and political life and the dynamics at work have been well-documented.[39] Because of cultural differences between the White majority and the Negro minority, the frequent exclusion of Negroes from socio-political life, the contemporary civil-rights ferment, and the less privileged position of Negroes in our society, it seems likely that redundant information would occur less often among Negro children. Therefore, the student sample was divided along racial lines.

Findings for the Negro Subsample

Although the Negro portion of the sample is not as large as one might wish (raw $N = 186$, weighted $N = 208$), it is sufficient to permit gross comparisons with White students of similar social characteristics and also to permit some analysis within the Negro sub-population. The subsample size and the fact that the dropout rate is appreciably higher among Negroes than Whites underscores the admonition that this subsample should not be extrapolated to the Negro age group in general. Also, the subsample contains twelve respondents classified as non-Whites other than Negro.

[39] In addition to such classic studies as Gunnar Myrdal's *An American Dilemma* (New York: Harper, 1944), see more recent works, Thomas F. Pettigrew, *A Profile of the American Negro* (Princeton: Van Nostrand, 1964); William Brink and Louis Harris, *The Negro Revolution in America* (New York: Simon and Schuster, 1964); Kenneth B. Clark, *Dark Ghetto* (New York: Harper and Row, 1965); Lewis Killian and Charles Grigg, *Racial Crises in America* (Englewood Cliffs: Prentice-Hall, 1964); Donald R. Matthews and James W. Prothro, *Negroes and the New Southern Politics* (New York: Harcourt, Brace and World, 1966); Dwaine Marvick, "The Political Socialization of the American Negro," *The Annals*, 361 (September, 1965), 112–27; and William C. Kvaraceus, *et al.*, *Negro Self-Concept: Implication for School and Citizenship* (New York: McGraw-Hill, 1965).

Demographically, a disproportionate number of the Negro students are located in the South (55 per cent *vs.* 25 per cent for Whites) and come from less advantaged backgrounds than Whites. This is true despite the fact that the backgrounds of Negro high school students are undoubtedly less deprived than those of their age group who dropped out. Social status differences between Negroes and Whites are more pronounced in the South than in the North.

Approximately the same proportions of Negro and White students have taken civics courses (Negroes 63 per cent, Whites 68 per cent). When the association between the curriculum and the dependent variables was re-examined within both racial groups, some intriguing differences caused us to reassess the place of the civics curriculum in the political socialization of American youth.

Political Knowledge

White students score higher on the knowledge scale than do Negroes, and when parents' education is controlled the differences persist at all levels. Civic courses have little effect on the absolute political knowledge level of Whites (beta = .08). The number of courses taken by Negroes, on the other hand, is significantly associated with their political knowledge score (beta = .30). The civics curriculum is an important source of political knowledge for Negroes and, as we shall see, appears in some cases to substitute for political information gathering in the media.

Although the multi-variate analysis holds parental education constant, it does not allow us to observe easily the singular role of this crucial socialization factor upon the relation between curriculum and political orientations. Therefore, contingency tables were constructed with parental education controlled for all relations between the number of government courses taken on the one hand, and each political orientation on the other. All instances in which education makes a distinctive imprint are reported.[40] For the case at hand—political

[40] Parental education was used as a summary control variable because we felt that it best captures the tone of the whole family environment, as well as other sources of socialization.

knowledge—controls for parental education did not alter the effects of the curriculum among either Whites or Negroes.

In another attempt to measure political knowledge as well as ideological sophistication, students were asked which political party they thought was most conservative or liberal. Each party has its "liberal" and "conservative" elements but studies of roll-call voting in Congress as well as the commentary of the politically aware places the Republican party somewhat to the right of the Democrats. Forty-five per cent of the students said that the Republicans were more conservative than the Democrats. Thirty-eight per cent did not know the answer.

In answering this question the student was faced with a problem not of his own making. It can be assumed that some respondents made a random choice (i.e., guessed) to extricate themselves. One gauge of the frequency of guessing is how often the Democrats were assigned a conservative position (17 per cent). If we make the reasonable assumption that this form of random choice is symmetric around the midpoint of the response dimension, we can say that an additional 17 per cent of the students guessed "correctly" when they put the Republicans in the conservative column. Accordingly, we may deduct 17 per cent from the 45 per cent who said Republicans were more conservative, leaving 28 per cent who are able to connect the conservative label to the Republican party.[41]

We are less interested in the absolute number of students who connected symbol with party than with the role the civics curriculum plays in this process. Again we see that course work has little impact on White students, while the per cent of Negroes who "know" the parties' ideological position increases as they take more courses (Table 4.2).

These findings, which use both measures of political knowledge, offer an excellent example of redundance. The clear inference as to why the Negro students' responses are "improved" by taking the courses is that new information is

[41] We have borrowed this method of adjusting "correct" answers from Donald E. Stokes, "Ideological Competition of British Parties," paper presented at 1964 Annual Meeting of the American Political Science Association, Chicago, Illinois.

being added where relatively little existed before. White students enrolled in the courses appear to receive nothing beyond that to which non-enrolled students are being exposed. This, coupled with the lead Whites have over Negro students in general, makes for greater redundancy among Whites.

TABLE 4.2. *Civics Curriculum and Knowing the Ideological Position of the Republican and Democratic Parties among Negro and White Students*

	ADJUSTED PERCENTAGE OF CORRECT RESPONSES			
Number of Civics Courses	Negro (per cent)	N	White (per cent)	N
0	0	(72)	29	(543)
1+	19	(122)	31	(1184)

One should not deduce that White students have a firm grasp on political knowledge. Table 4.2 and other data indicate that they clearly do not. Rather, White students apparently have reached a saturation level which is impervious to change by the civics curriculum. Because Negroes have started at a relatively lower position, their knowledge level is increased by exposure to the civics curriculum.

Political Efficacy and Political Cynicism

Almost twice as many Negro students as Whites scored low on the political efficacy scale. When the effect of parental education is partialed out, the racial differences remain at each educational level, although they are somewhat diminished. It is interesting that the difference in the percentage of those who scored low is less between Negro and White students whose parents have had only an elementary school education (13 per cent) than between Negro and White students whose parents have had a college education (24 per cent).

The number of civics courses taken by White students has little perceptible effect on their sense of political efficacy (beta = .05). Among Negroes, however, course exposure is moderately related to a sense of efficacy (beta = .18). As seen in Table 4.3, this is particularly true for Negroes from less educated families. The strength of the relationship decreases significantly among higher-status students. Course-taking among the lower-status Negroes brings their scores into line with their higher-status cohorts. There is only a faint trace of this pattern among White students.

TABLE 4.3. *Number of Civics Courses Taken and Political Efficacy among Negro Students, by Parental Education*

NUMBER OF CIVICS COURSES[a]	ELEMENTARY SCHOOL POLITICAL EFFICACY				
	Low (per cent)	Medium (per cent)	High (per cent)	N	Gamma
0	64	20	16	18	
1+	30	27	43	39	.56
	HIGH SCHOOL POLITICAL EFFICACY				
	Low (per cent)	Medium (per cent)	High (per cent)	N	Gamma
0	56	20	24	41	
1+	34	27	39	62	.36
	COLLEGE POLITICAL EFFICACY				
	Low (per cent)	Medium (per cent)	High (per cent)	N	Gamma
0	32	32	36	15	
1+	37	19	44	24	.02

[a] Parental education was set by the highest level achieved by either parent. "Elementary" means neither parent exceeded an eighth-grade education; "high school" means at least one parent had one or more years of high school training; and "college" means at least one parent had one or more years of college experience.

Although Negro students at all levels of parental education feel less efficacious than their White counterparts, it must be concluded that without the civics curriculum the gap would be even greater. Again, we have another illustration of less redundancy at work among the Negro subsample. For a variety of reasons the American political culture produces a lower sense of efficacy among Negro youths. By heavily emphasizing the legitimacy, desirability, and feasibility of citizen participation and control, the civics course adds a new element in the socialization of low- and middle-status Negro students. Since those from the less educated families are more likely to be surrounded by agents with generally low efficacy levels, the curriculum has considerably more effect. Leaving aside possible later disappointments in testing the reality of their new-found efficacy, the Negro students from less privileged backgrounds are, for the moment, visibly moved by course exposure.

While Negroes as a whole are less politically efficacious than Whites, they are not at the same time more politically cynical. The proportion of twelfth graders falling into the three most cynical categories of a six-point political cynicism scale includes 21 per cent of the White and 23 per cent of the Negro students. This relatively low level of political cynicism among Negroes may seem ironic, but it is consistent with their view of the "good citizen" role (discussed later pp. 109–13). The high school civics curriculum has only a slight effect upon the cynicism level of Whites (beta $= .11$) and none on Negroes (beta $= -.01$). However, this difference suggests that the cynicism of Negroes may be somewhat less moveable.

Civic Tolerance

One of the abiding goals of civic education is the encouragement of civic toleration. Negroes as a whole score lower on the civic tolerance scale than do Whites. When parental education is controlled, the racial differences remain at each education level, although they are moderately attenuated. Again, as with political efficacy, the differences in the percentage of those scoring low is least between Negro and White students whose parents have had only an elementary school education (18 per cent) and most between Negro and White students whose parents have had a college education (28 per cent). What we may be witnessing is the result of Negro compensation for the White bias in American society—a bias to which higher-status Negroes may prove most sensitive.

The number of civics courses taken has little effect on White students' civic tolerance scores (beta = .06), although there is somewhat greater impact on those from homes of lower parental education. There is, however, a moderate association between exposure and Negro students' sense of civic tolerance (beta = .22). The more courses they take, the higher their level of tolerance. Negroes are more intolerant even when educational controls are introduced, but the civics curriculum appears to overcome in part the environmental factors which may contribute to their relatively lower tolerance. The items on which the civic-tolerance measure is based all concern the acceptance of diversity. Aggregate student and parent data suggest that these items tap a dimension of political sophistication less likely to be operative in the Negro-sub-culture. To the extent that the civics courses preach more tolerance, the message is less likely to be repetitious among Negroes than Whites. Unlike political knowledge and efficacy, however, course-taking exerts its main effect on Negro twelfth graders from better educated families, thereby suggesting that a threshold of receptivity may be lacking among those from lower-status families.

Politicization—Interest, Discussion, and Media Usage

Students were asked about their interest in public affairs and how often they discussed politics with their friends outside class. There is little difference between racial groups among those who expressed high interest in politics or said they discussed politics weekly or more often with their friends. Nor did controls for parental education uncover aggregate racial distinctions. Moreover, the civics curriculum appears at first glance to have little impact upon these two indicators of politicization among Negroes (beta = .15 and − .07, respectively) or Whites (beta = .06 and .04). Yet, as Table 4.4 indicates, curriculum effect is differentially determined by the educational level of the Negro students' parents (in contrast to a lack of variation found among

Whites). The differential effect may account for the low beta coefficient in the multi-variate analysis.

TABLE 4.4. *Gamma Correlation between Number of Civics Courses Taken and Political Interest and Discussion with Peers among Negro Students, by Parental Education*

Parental Education	Political Interest	Political Discussion
Elementary	+.31	+.20
High School	−.18	−.31
College	−.21	−.36

As Negroes from less educated families take more civics courses their political interest and frequency of political discussion with peers increases. Since less educated parents ordinarily are less politicized, one could explain this in terms of non-redundant information spurring an increase in their children's politicization. Students from higher-status families, however, actually appear to undergo *depoliticization* as they move through the civics curriculum.

In their excellent inquiry into the personality of the American Negro, Abram Kardiner and Lionel Ovesey observed that the higher-status Negro is most likely to identify and have contact with Whites and their culture.[42] But because of his race, disappointments are frequent and aspirations likely to founder on the rock of unattainable ideals.

Because of his parents' experience, the higher-status Negro student may receive a more "realistic" appraisal of the social restrictions placed upon Negro participation in the United States. In the civics course he finds at least two good-citizen roles emphasized. The first stresses politicized-participation; the second emphasizes a more passive role: loyalty and obedience to authority and nation. If he has absorbed from his parents the probability of restrictions, the participation-politicization emphasis in the curriculum may have little impact

[42] Abram Kardiner and Lionel Ovesey, *The Mark of Oppression* (Cleveland: World, 1962).

on the higher-status Negro student. The "reality factor" causes him to select out of the curriculum only those role characteristics which appear to be congruent with a preconceived notion of his political life chances. As we shall see later, higher-status Negro students' perception of the good-citizen role is compatible with this interpretation.

Students were also asked how often they read articles in newspapers or magazines or watched programs on television about public affairs, news, or politics. In the aggregate, students from each racial grouping employ newspapers and magazines at about the same rate; but Negro students at all levels of parental education look at television more often than Whites. The civics curriculum has a different impact upon how Whites and Negroes use political media. Table 4.5 shows that for White students there is a consistent—but very weak—association between taking civics courses and using media as an access point to political information, while among Negroes a consistently negative but somewhat stronger association exists.

TABLE 4.5. *Partial Beta Coefficients between Number of Civics Courses Taken and Political Media Usage among Negro and White Students*

Media	Negro	White
Newspapers	−.17	+.07
Television	−.21	+.04
Magazines	−.10	+.10

Observing the same relationship within contingency tables under less severe control conditions, the civics curriculum continues to have a negative—although fluctuating—impact upon political media usage among Negroes at *all* levels of parental education (Table 4.6).

Negative correlations among Negroes might be explained on at least two dimensions: substitution and depoliticization. A civics course may increase a student's political interest, while at the same time acting as a substitute for political information-gathering in the media. This appears to be happening among Negroes from less educated families. Negative associations between course work and media usage suggest that the former may be substituting for political information-gathering in the media. But as we saw before, there is a significant increase in political interest among lower-status Negroes as they take more civics courses. The absence of depoliticization in this group was further confirmed by the positive correlation between the civics curriculum and discussing politics with one's school friends (Table 4.4).

TABLE 4.6. *Gamma Correlations between Number of Civics Courses Taken and Political Media Usage among Negro Students, by Parental Education*

	PARENTAL EDUCATION		
Media	*Primary*	*Secondary*	*College*
Newspapers	−.07	−.36	−.28
Television	−.39	−.42	−.17
Magazines	−.27	−.07	−.42

The case of the higher-status Negro seems to be different. Negative correlations between the civics curriculum and media usage may indicate substitution, but what is even more apparent is the general depoliticization of higher-status Negroes as they move through the curriculum. The more courses they take the less likely they are to seek political information in newspapers, magazines, and television. In addition there is a decrease in their political interest and propensity to discuss politics with their friends.

Citizenship Behavior

Interjecting race adds a special complexity to the relationship between the civics curriculum and the student's belief about the role of a good citizen in this country. Students were asked, "People have different ideas about what being a good citizen means. We're interested in what you think. Tell me how you would describe a good citizen in this country—that is, what things about a person are most important in showing that he is a good citizen."

Taking only their first responses, 70 per cent of the Whites and 63 per cent of the Negroes fell along two general dimensions: loyalty and political participation. Within these, there are distinct racial differences. Sixty-one per cent of the Negro responses focus on loyalty rather than participation. Only 40 per cent of the White students, on the other hand, see the "good-citizen" role as one of loyalty rather than political participation. When we probe the relation between taking civic courses and citizenship orientation, some interesting differences are revealed. More civics courses mean more loyalty and less participation-orientation for Negroes. Table 4.7 shows a 24 per cent difference in loyalty orientation between Negroes who have taken no civic courses and those who have taken one or more. These courses have a slightly opposite effect among White students.

TABLE 4.7. *Civics Curriculum and Good Citizenship Attitudes among Negro and White Students*

	NEGROES STRESSING:		
Number of Civics Courses	Loyalty (per cent)	Participation (per cent)	N[a]
0	51	49	41
1+	75	25	85

	WHITES STRESSING:		
	Loyalty (per cent)	Participation (per cent)	
0	46	54	395
1+	39	61	803

[a] These N's run lower than corresponding N's in other tables because those respondents who did not mention either loyalty or participation in their first response are excluded.

In other words, while the civics curriculum has little impact upon the White student's view of the good-citizen role, it appears to inculcate in Negroes the expectation that a good citizen is above all a loyal citizen, rather than an active one. Yet, looking at this same relationship among Negroes under the more severe multi-variate control conditions, the size of the beta coefficient ($-.10$) is not large.[43] Even though it is predictably negative (i.e., loyalty orientation increases with course work), the magnitude of the coefficient reduces our confidence in the earlier contingency table.

The difference in findings may be the result of moving from a relatively simple bivariate analysis with no controls for other possible intervening variables to a more sophisticated multi-variate analysis under more rigorously controlled conditions. But also we found, as before, that the differential effect of the civics curriculum upon Negroes depends on the educational level of their parents.

TABLE 4.8. *Civics Curriculum and Citizenship Attitudes among Negro Students, by Parental Education*

NUMBER OF CIVICS COURSES	ELEMENTARY		
	Loyalty (*per cent*)	*Participation* (*per cent*)	*N*
0	83	17	6
1+	63	37	28
	HIGH SCHOOL		
	Loyalty	*Participation*	
0	54	46	24
1+	90	10	41
	COLLEGE		
	Loyalty	*Participation*	
0	32	68	11
1+	60	40	17

Negro students whose parents have some secondary school or college education increase their loyalty orientation by 36

[43] The beta coefficient for White students is $+.07$.

per cent and 28 per cent, respectively, as they take more civics courses (Table 4.8). Negroes from less educated families, however, increase their participation-orientation much like White students. Due to the small N for Negro students who have taken no courses and whose parents have only an elementary school education or less, this relationship should be treated with caution. Although the pattern has a theoretically compelling consistency with the differences found previously between Negroes from different levels of parental education, the most one would want to say here is that the civics curriculum seems to increase the loyalty orientations of higher-status Negroes, while having a slightly opposite effect among lower-status Negro students.

A number of interpretations can be placed on these findings. Both loyalty and participation are emphasized in the civics curriculum, and for White and lower-status Negro students the dual emphasis has nearly equal effect. But, as we noted earlier, the higher-status Negro may have received from his more active parents a "realistic" appraisal of the restrictions placed upon Negro participation in American politics. Consequently, the participation emphasis in the curriculum has little impact.

Another rationale for the findings might be found in the relative fulfillment of White and Negro "needs to belong," to be accepted in the society. If we assume that the Negro is cut off from many of the associational memberships and status advantages most Whites take for granted, then his unfulfilled need to be accepted is probably greater than that of his White counterparts. This may be particularly true of the higher-status Negro and his parents. Because of their relatively higher education in the Negro community, they have had more contacts with Whites—contacts which, because of their race, have led to more frequent rebuffs. The one association not explicitly denied Negroes is that of being a loyal American. It is entirely possible that the psychic relief a higher-status Negro receives in "establishing" his American good citizenship is greater than that of his White counterpart or his lower-status racial peer. As a consequence, the loyalty emphasis in the curriculum may have the most impact on the higher-status Negro.[44]

Regional Effects

Negro students are located disproportionately in the southern part of the United States. Because of possible cultural differences we decided to control for region as well as for parental education. Therefore the Negro subsample was divided into South and non-South with controls for high and low parental education in each region.[45]

When controlled for region as well as parental education, the effects of the civics curriculum upon political knowledge, interest, discussion, television-newspaper-magazine usage, and loyalty-participation orientations were consistent with the results for the Negro subsample as a whole, with only two exceptions. Among the seven variables discussed above, there are 28 cases (two for each region because of the education control, or four for each variable) in which a possible deviation from the Negro subsample as a whole could occur. Be-

[44] In 1942 Gunnar Myrdal completed a comprehensive codification of the Negro culture and circumstances in America. He maintained that Negroes in this country were "exaggerated Americans," who believed in the American creed more strongly than did Whites. Gunnar Myrdal, *An American Dilemma.*

[45] The Negro subsample was not large to begin with, and a regional control in addition to the control for parental education reduced cell frequencies even further. Because the differential effects of parental education were found primarily between students whose parents had only an elementary school education versus those with high school or college education, we combined students from the latter two categories into one category. This retained the substance of the original education break in the South, but it still left only a small number of students outside the South whose parents had an elementary school education or less. In order to enlarge this latter group the parental education cutting point in the non-South was moved to a point between those parents who were at least high school graduates and those who had only some high school or less. If there are important regional differences in curriculum effect they should be apparent under these control conditions. The respective raw and weighted N's for the four groups are as follows: southern low educated—39,44; southern high educated—63,64; non-southern low educated—53,42; non-southern high educated—59,50.

cause of the small marginals, and the fact that there were 26 consistent findings, we attach little significance to these two exceptions.

In both regions, the civics curriculum continued to be negatively associated with political media usage at all educational levels, except for newspaper reading among higher-status students outside the South. The relationships are slightly stronger in the South. The differential consequences of parental education were remarkably consistent across both regions. As before, civics courses had a negative effect upon political discussion (and political interest in the South) among higher-status Negroes while having a positive impact upon lower-status Negroes. Finally, in both regions the civics curriculum continued to have its greatest negative effect on the participatory orientations of Negro students from the more educated families.

There appeared to be different regional effects on only three of the dependent variables. The first of these was political cynicism. In the South, course work slightly increases cynicism among high- and low-status Negroes, while in the North political cynicism decreased as the student was exposed to the civics curriculum. In both regions, however, taking a civics course makes the student from the higher educated family relatively more cynical than his lower-status peer. As with cynicism, exposure to civics means a slight decrease in civic tolerance among high- and low-status southern Negroes. This is also true of lower-status Negroes outside the South. For all three cases, the magnitude of the relationships is quite small, the highest being a gamma of $-.14$. Only among higher status non-southern Negroes is a stronger, positive relationship found— $+.39$.

The political efficacy of lower-status students in the South was increased much more by the civics curriculum (.64) than was the efficacy of their higher-status peers (.32). This is consistent with the picture for the entire subsample. However, while there was a positive relation between exposure and increased efficacy among higher-status students in the non-South there was a negative relationship among lower-status students. We are at a loss to explain this negative sign other than point to the small frequencies which may account for this departure.

Summary and Conclusion

A number of studies in the United States and other countries have stressed the importance of education in determining political attitudes and behavior. The man with only a primary school education is a different political actor from the individual who has gone to high school or college. Yet direct evidence demonstrating the effect of college and high school curriculum upon political beliefs and behavior of students is scarce.

Our findings certainly do not support the thinking of those who look to the civics curriculum in American high schools as even a minor source of political socialization. When we investigated the student sample as a whole, we found not one single case out of the ten examined in which the civics curriculum was significantly associated with students' political orientations.

The lack of positive results raised many questions concerning the simple correlations between years of education and political orientations which are so prevalent in the literature, particularly the differences between people with high school versus college education. Of course, high schools and colleges are complex institutions. While the formal curriculum may have little effect, the acquisition of conceptual skills, the social climate of the school, and the presence of peer groups all may play a significant role in the political socialization process.[46] Still, these caveats overlook one of the chief difficulties in studying the influence of higher education: *the danger of confounding the effect of selection with that of socialization.* For example, do the highly educated feel more politically competent because of their college socialization experiences or were they significantly different in this respect

---

[46] See Almond and Verba, *The Civic Culture,* chap. 12; and M. L. Levin, "Social Climates and Political Socialization," *Public Opinion Quarterly,* 25 (Winter, 1961), 596–606.

from their non-college bound peers before they entered college?

College bound students do differ significantly from those who are not planning on college. They tend to come from families with above-average incomes and education and possess the cultural benefits of their higher status.[47] We found among high school seniors a strong positive correlation between parents' education and students' intention to attend a four-year college or university ($\gamma = .52$). Because there was also a strong correlation between high school grades ($\gamma = .53$) and college intentions, we feel confident that stated intention to attend college is a fairly good predictor of future attendance.

The fact that college bound students enjoy higher social status than their non-college bound peers suggests that there also may be important political differences between the two groups. Indeed, students who plan to attend college are more likely to be knowledgeable about politics ($\gamma = .39$), to express greater political interest (.32) and efficacy (.37), to support religious dissenters' rights of free speech (.37) and an elected communist's right to take public office (.44), to read about politics in newspapers (.18) and magazines (.34), and to discuss politics with their peers (.26). Moreover, they are three times as likely to place the correct liberal-conservative label on the Democratic and Republican parties, compared with students not planning to pursue a college education.

To summarize, there is a lack of evidence that the civics curriculum has a significant effect on the political orientations of the great majority of American high school students. Moreover, those who are college bound already have different political orientations than those who are not. These two conclusions suggest that an important part of the difference in political orientations between those from different levels of education, which is frequently cited in the literature and is usually explicitly or implicitly ascribed to the "education

[47] Ernest Haveman and Patricia West, *They Went to College* (New York: Harcourt), 1952.

process," may actually represent a serious confounding of the effect of selection with that of political socialization.

Although the overall findings are unambiguous, under special conditions exposure to government and politics courses has an impact at the secondary-school level. When White and Negro students were observed separately, it became clear that the curriculum exerted considerably more influence on the latter. On several measures the effect was to move the Negro youths to a position more congruent with the White youths and with the usual goals of civic education in the United States. Negroes who have taken one or more civics courses were found to have more political knowledge and ideological sophistication, a greater sense of political efficacy, and a higher level of civic tolerance than those who had taken no courses.

In a number of cases, curriculum effect was strongly influenced by the educational level of the Negro student's parents, with its greatest positive impact occurring among the lower classes. For example, the strongest association between course work and political efficacy was among Negroes from lower-status families. The civics curriculum was also related to increased political interest and discussion among these students whose parents had less than a high school education.

The relationships were increasingly complex for Negroes with more educated parents. For example, differences in efficacy levels between White and Negro students were greatest among those from families with the most educated parents. Moreover, the civics curriculum had no effect upon the development of a sense of efficacy among these high-status Negroes. These findings took on greater meaning when we found that enrollment in civics courses was *negatively associated* with political interest and discussion among higher-status Negroes while increasing their relative political cynicism. In addition, civics was negatively associated with political media usage for this group. Negative correlations for media usage were also true for lower-status Negroes. But in this case, civics courses appeared to be substituting for political information gathering in the media, while at the same time stimulating political interest and discussion. For higher-status Negroes, however, the consistent negative correlations across *all* the indicators of politicization underscores that depoliticization may be as important a factor as substitution for this group.

A number of reasons were given for these findings. What we may be witnessing is the unfortunate result of Negro compensation for the White bias in American society—a bias to which higher-status Negroes and their parents are most sensitive. Higher-status Negroes are more likely to identify and have contact with the White community. But due to their race, the rebuffs and disappointments are more frequent. Because of their parents' experiences, these students may receive a more "realistic" appraisal of the restrictions placed upon Negro participation in the United States. If they enroll in a civics course and find a politicized-participant citizenship role being stressed, as well as a more passive role of loyalty and obedience to authority and nation, they may select out of the curriculum those role characteristics which conform best to the reality of their parents' experiences.

This interpretation is consistent with the effect of the civics curriculum upon the perception of the good-citizenship role held by Negroes from more educated families. Negroes in general are more likely than Whites to see loyalty, rather than participation, as being most important to good citizenship. However, those students from families with a high school or college education increase their loyalty orientation as they take more civics courses, while Negroes from the least educated families are more likely to view good citizenship as consonant with participation.

One explanation of the singular consequence of the curriculum upon Negro students is that information redundancy is lower for them than for White students. Because of cultural and social status differences, Negro students are more likely to encounter new or conflicting perspectives and content. The more usual case for Whites is a further layering of familiar materials which, by and large, repeat information from other sources.

It is conceivable that other sub-populations of students are also differently affected by the curriculum, that variations in content and pedagogy lead to varying outcomes, or that delayed consequences result from course exposure. In the main, however, one is hard pressed to find evidence of any immediate impact of courses on the bulk of students. The programmatic implications of this conclusion are forceful. If the educational system continues to invest sizable resources in civics courses at the secondary level—as seems probable—these courses must be reconstructed if they are to show appreciable pay-off. Changes in goals, course content, pedagogy, timing of exposure, teacher training, and school environmental factors are all points of leverage. Until such changes come about, one can expect little contribution from the formal civics curriculum in the political socialization of American youth.

We should note, however, that in transitional societies traditional norms often clash with the modern values being inculcated in the schools. If under these conditions elites are interested in rapid development and political change, they may depend heavily upon the conscious manipulation of the formal as well as the informal environment of the school.[48] Yet within school systems where self-conscious indoctrination does not take a massive form, and formal instruction results in greater information redundancy, there is little evidence that curriculum will have a significant effect on the political values of students.

[48] Stephen Dunn and Ethel Dunn, "Directed Cultural Change in the Soviet Union: Some Soviet Studies," *American Anthropologist,* 64 (April, 1962), 328–39; Urie Bronfenbrenner, "Soviet Methods of Character Education," *American Psychologist,* 17 (August, 1962), 550–64; and Franklin Houn, *To Change a Nation* (New York: Free Press, 1961).

CHAPTER FIVE

THE INFORMAL MILIEU:
PEER GROUP AND SCHOOL

▌▌▌▌▌ The inconclusive findings and general lack of evidence concerning the political impact of the formal school environment has led many students of socialization to a closer examination of the less formal milieu of the school.[1]

In this chapter we examine the impact of the class climate in peer groups and schools upon the reinforcement or change of political attitudes and behavior patterns.

The major questions are:

1. What is the relation between the class homogeneity-heterogeneity of peer groups and schools and the isolation of lower class students from the political and economic norms of higher class students? For example, do homogeneous class peer groups and schools reinforce the political culture of the working class while heterogeneous class environments tend to re-socialize lower class students in the direction of norms held by students of higher class status?

2. Does the heterogeneous class climate of both peer group and school have a cumulative effect on the re-socialization of working class political attitudes and behavior patterns?

---

[1] James S. Coleman (ed.), *Education and Political Development* (Princeton: Princeton University Press, 1965), pp. 18–25; Martin L. Levin, "Social Climates and Political Socialization," *Public Opinion Quarterly,* 25 (Winter, 1961), 596–606; David Riesman, *Faces in the Crowd* (New Haven: Yale University Press, 1952), p. 559; Theodore M. Newcomb, *Personality and Social Change* (New York: Dryden Press, 1943); and David Ziblatt, "High School Extra Curricular Activities and Political Socialization," *The Annals,* 361 (September, 1965), 21–31.

3. What are the cross-cultural implications of these findings for the conscious manipulation of the school environment?

While these questions are sufficiently broad to be amenable to empirical testing in any political culture in which class cleavages exist, the primary source of data here is the Caribbean student sample and comparative data from a survey of 1349 primary and secondary school students in Detroit, Michigan.[2]

Before turning to these questions it is important to note that the socializing influence of the peer group and school milieu may itself be affected by early family socialization.[3] For example, Chapter 2 showed that respondents from authoritarian families are more likely to deviate from family party preferences and to identify with those of their peers than are respondents from less authoritarian families. When the influence of family structure is examined, we see that students from maternal families are appreciably more outgroup oriented[4] in seeking political advice and in whom they think most influenced their political opinions than are respondents from nuclear families (Table 5.1).

Apparently students from the less politicized maternal family must seek political advice outside of the family, because the mother has less time for politics due to her increased economic responsibilities.

Before discussing peer group and school, a final example illustrates how different family environments may pre-

[2] I wish to thank Roberta S. Sigel and Irving S. Sigel for the use of their data which was gathered from selected Detroit secondary and primary schools in 1964 during their study of school children's reactions to the assassination of President Kennedy. See Roberta S. Sigel, "An Exploration into Some Aspects of Political Socialization: School Children's Reaction to the Death of a President," in Martha Wolfenstein and Gilbert Kliman (eds.), *Children and the Death of a President* (Garden City: Doubleday, 1965), pp. 30–61.

[3] Charles E. Bowerman and John W. Kinch, "Changes in Family and Peer Orientations of Children between the Fourth and Tenth Grades," *Social Forces,* 37 (March, 1959), 206–11.

[4] Outgroups consist primarily of peer groups, school teachers, and a miscellaneous assortment of "others."

condition the impact of these intermediary agencies. Students were asked, "How much do you think your parents' social position [i.e., their station in life] will hurt your chances for success?" It was hypothesized that an individual who feels that the social status of his family impedes his own chances for success is more likely to turn away from his family and to be influenced politically by his school peer group than a respondent who is less alienated.

TABLE 5.1. *Family Structure and Outgroup Political Orientations among Jamaican Secondary School Students*

FAMILY STRUCTURE	TO WHOM WOULD YOU GO FOR POLITICAL ADVICE ON VOTING?		
	Family (per cent)	Outgroups (per cent)	N
Nuclear Family	71	29	417
Maternal Family	51	49	83

	WHO HAS HAD THE MOST INFLUENCE ON YOUR POLITICAL OPINIONS?		
	Family (per cent)	Outgroups (per cent)	N
Nuclear Family	61	39	297
Maternal Family	28	72	53

TABLE 5.2 *Alienation from Family Social Status and Relative Political Influence of Peer Group and Family*

FAMILY ALIENATION	POLITICAL INFLUENCE OF:		
	Family (per cent)	Peer Group (per cent)	N
Very Much	52	48	44
Somewhat	63	37	73
A Little	64	36	143
None	67	33	369

Subjective perceptions of influence on the part of the respondent are used as an index of the relative influence of the family and peer group upon students' political opinions. The influence of the peer group increases uniformly with the strength of the individual's alienation from his family (Table 5.2). Thus as reaction against what is felt to be the disadvantageous social status of one's family increases, the influence of the peer group over the political opinions of the respondent also increases, while that of his family is attenuated.

Peer Group

The influence of the group upon the perceptions and opinions of an individual is one of the better documented generalizations in small group literature.[5] Because peer groups provide a student with a feeling of integration and help him adjust to school life, they tend to make his opinions subject to their influence.[6] Studies have documented the influence of high school peer groups on social norms and aspirations, school achievement, and so forth.[7] Many scholars have concluded that the student culture is one of the prime educational forces at work in the schools, and that assimilation into it is the primary concern of most students.[8] There has been little empirical research, however, on the impact of peer groups on political orientations. Peter Rose did show that during the 1956 election Cornell University students who had friends for Stevenson voted for the Democratic candidate

[5] James C. Davies, *Human Nature in Politics* (New York: Wiley, 1963), pp. 170–72; Sidney Verba, *Small Groups and Political Behavior* (Princeton: Princeton University Press, 1961), pp. 22–23, 90–109; Robert Lane and David Sears, *Public Opinion* (Englewood Cliffs: Prentice-Hall, 1964), pp. 33–42.

[6] Theodore Newcomb, "Student Peer Group Influence," in Robert Sutherland, *et al.*, *Personality Factors on the College Campus* (Austin: Hogg Foundation, 1962), p. 69.

[7] James S. Coleman, *The Adolescent Society* (New York: Free Press, 1961), and August Hollingshead, *Elmtown's Youth* (New York: Wiley, 1949).

[8] Nevitt Sanford (ed.), *The American College* (New York: Knopf, 1963), and Newcomb and Wilson, *College Peer Groups.*

two to one, and those with friends for Eisenhower voted for him three to one; both proportions were significantly larger than the vote of the total student body.[9] In the classic study conducted at Bennington College, Theodore Newcomb demonstrated that college peers, or, more accurately, prestige groups,[10] may play an important role in the political resocialization process.[11]

Yet, perhaps one of the foremost functions of peer groups is to transmit the culture of the wider society of which they are a part. While student peer groups may have a sub-culture of their own, they also teach the adult sub-culture of which they are a part and reinforce the norms and social patterns held by adult society.[12] Social class, and religious and ethnic sub-cultures are transmitted through the peer group. A child who grows up in a working class family learns the working class way of life. If he enters a school peer group composed of students from the same social class, this may act to reinforce as well as elaborate the class attitudes and expectations already learned in the family.

In addition to its function of transmitting or reinforcing the political culture of the society, the peer group may provide a social system in which the individual learns new attitudes and behavior. For example, the peer group with a homogeneous class composition operates to reinforce its particular class way of life and political orientations, but a lower class boy or girl entering a heterogeneous class peer group in which he interacts with individuals of higher social status may learn new ways of behaving and believing.

Children begin early to distinguish between subordinate and superordinate statuses and to associate rewards and pun-

[9] Peter Rose, "Student Opinion on the 1956 Presidential Election," *Public Opinion Quarterly*, 21 (1957), 371–76.

[10] Unfortunately, peer group is a term frequently used without definition or with multiple definitions. It does not always refer to a primary or face-to-face group, but often refers to age, grade, and social class cohorts. In this study peer group refers to a face-to-face group of "best friends."

[11] Newcomb, *Personality and Social Change.*

[12] Robert J. Havighurst and Bernice L. Neugarten, *Society and Education* (Boston: Allyn and Bacon, 1962), 2nd ed., chap. 5.

ishments with particular patterns of imitation. Social classes have their characteristic stigmata, which constitute a similar set of cues for lower class groups.[13] The literature suggests that higher-status peers become especially significant as models for identification. For they are in a position to reward peer group members of lesser status by bestowing approval, attention, leadership, or by giving permission to participate in peer activities or to employ certain symbols. Harvey and Rutherford found that American students in heterogeneous class peer groups changed their opinions in the direction of those held by high-status peers. However, this shift was greater in higher (sixth–eleventh grades) than in the lower grades. The development of class consciousness may be a corollary of the maturation process.[14] Remmers and Radler found in their national sample of American high school students that respondents from low income homes were more likely to defer to the opinions of their peers on racial questions than were students from medium and high income homes. Low income students were also much more likely to follow the dictates of their peers, rather than to suggest new group activity.[15]

Interestingly enough, Cecil Stendler discovered that out-of-school peer groups were generally more class-homogeneous, while there was a greater tendency for peer groups within the school to cross class lines.[16] This suggests that the environment of the school peer group may be more conducive to re-socialization than informal peer groups outside the school.

From this, we might hypothesize that the primary function of homogeneous class peer groups in the political so-

[13] Neal Miller and John Dollard, *Social Learning and Imitation* (New Haven: Yale University Press, 1941), pp. 188–93.

[14] J. Harvey and J. M. Rutherford, "Status in the Informal Group: Influence and Influencibility at Different Age Levels," *Child Development*, 31 (June, 1960), 377–85.

[15] H. H. Remmers and D. H. Radler, *The American Teenager* (New York: Bobbs-Merrill, 1957), pp. 234–37.

[16] Cecil B. Stendler, *Children of Brasstown* (Urbana: Bureau of Research and Service of the College of Education, University of Illinois, 1949).

cialization process is to reinforce the way of life and associated political orientations of the lower classes, and thus, to maintain the political and cultural cleavages which may exist between the classes. On the other hand, heterogeneous class peer groups function in an important way to re-socialize the attitudes of working class members in the direction of those held by higher class peers.

Class Differences

A consistent pattern of political cleavages exists among the different social strata in Jamaican society.[17] In light of research findings in the United States on the relation between objective class and political attitudes, we are not surprised to find that working class students in Jamaica are less committed to the values of a "democratic" order, less supportive of the civil liberties of Jamaican minority groups, less positively oriented toward voting, and less politicized than the middle and upper classes.[18] The relationships are monotonic

[17] The respondent's social class is determined by his position on an index composed of two items: the occupation of his father and the education of his mother or father—whichever is higher.

[18] It has generally been found that working class Americans have a lesser sense of citizenship duty and less disposition to vote than those from higher social classes. Robert E. Lane, *Political Life* (Glencoe: Free Press, 1959), pp. 157–60.

In our analysis of data concerning the effects of the civics curriculum upon American high school seniors (Chapter 4), we found students from less educated families scored lower in civil tolerance and were less politicized than those from more educated parents. H. H. Remmers, and Remmers and Radler also found that American high school students from the lower classes were less politicized, less tolerant of civil liberties, and less disposed toward the norms of a "democratic" order than were higher class students. See *Purdue Opinion Poll*, Number 30, November, 1951; and Remmers and Radler, *The American Teenager*, chap. 8.

The reader should note that the degree of class polarization on comparable political attitudes and issues can be expected to vary between countries. Moreover, it has been demonstrated that the degree of class polarization within a country is likely to vary over time. Philip E. Converse, "The Shifting Role of Class" in E. Hartley, *Readings in Social Psychology* (New York: Holt, 1958), 3rd ed., pp. 388–99.

in all cases; the working and upper classes occupy opposite ends of the various indices.[19]

We also attempted to ascertain the respondents' general orientation toward the political system as a whole. This diffuse system affect is likely to vary between political cultures and more important, for our purposes, negative and positive affect may vary between social classes. Almond and Verba found, for example, that in the United States, Great Britain, and Mexico, the better educated respondents and those with higher status occupations were more likely to express general pride in their respective political systems than were those from lesser statuses.[20]

In contrast, we find in Jamaica an increase in positive affect or "support" and a decrease in ambivalence as social class decreases.[21] There appears to be no relation between class and negative affect or "opposition" to the political system (Table 5.3).

The relatively strong support and less political cynicism found among the working class may be explained in terms of appeals to class and the charismatic nature of Jamaican poli-

[19] Respondents were asked to express their opinions on the following:
1. General "democratic" orientation: "Economic security is more important than political freedom."
2. Attitude toward voting: "It won't matter much to me if I vote or not when I become an adult."
3. Civil Liberties: "Rastafarians (Jamaican minority group) should not be allowed to hold public meetings even if they gather peacefully and only make speeches."
4. Politicization: Respondents' placement on this index was determined by the frequency in which they discussed politics with members of the family, school friends, teachers, or politicians; and the frequency in which they read political articles in the national newspaper.
The differences between the position of the working class and the upper class on each of these four variables was 15, 12, 13 and 13 per cent, respectively.

[20] Gabriel Almond and Sidney Verba, *The Civic Culture*, p. 105.

[21] Respondents were asked: "Do you feel politics and the government have been honest, dishonest, neither honest nor dishonest?" This question might also be considered a measure of general political cynicism.

tics. Both political parties in Jamaica have attempted to project the charisma of their respective leaders before the working class Jamaican. Most successful political campaigns combined charisma with "bread and butter" trade union appeals directed primarily at the working class. While the lower classes may have found both of these appeals and the tone of Jamaican politics particularly attractive, this has only tended to make the more educated classes increasingly suspicious of "mob appeal" and intolerant of alleged corruption and waste.

TABLE 5.3. *Relation of Social Class to System Legitimacy*

SOCIAL CLASS	SYSTEM LEGITIMACY			
	Support (per cent)	Ambivalent (per cent)	Oppose (per cent)	N
Working Class	40	46	14	462
Middle Class	33	53	14	272
Upper Class	28	55	17	338

Students were also asked to give their opinions on certain economic issues. Some of these issues impinge directly on class prerogatives.[22] Generally the findings conform to the well-documented proposition that the lower class is less economically "conservative" than the higher class.

Although class polarization on the preceding political and economic issues is not as dramatic in Jamaica as it might be in other societies, given the consistent pattern of political cleavages that exists among the different social strata, we hypothesized that peer groups and schools play an important role in reinforcing or re-socializing the political and economic attitudes of the working class. (The case of the middle and upper class student will be discussed later in this chapter.)

[22] The questions were as follows:
1. "Do you think the rich should give up their privileges?"
2. "Should there be some upper limit, such as 10,000 pounds a year, on how much any one person can earn?"

Peer Class Environment
and Political Socialization

The class homogeneity-heterogeneity of the respondent's peer group was based on his own perception of the peer environment. We asked respondents if their best friends in school were in the same social class as they or in a different one. Type of house and amount of money were given as criteria of class indices. Students who responded "the same social class" were categorized as being members of homogeneous class peer groups. Those who responded that their best school friends were from "higher, lower, as well as the same social class" were categorized as being members of heterogenous class peer groups. If, for example, a respondent had an objective working class status and he said that his best friends in school were members of the same social class, then for the purposes of this study, that school peer group is considered to be of a generally homogeneous working class nature.

There may be some systematic distortion in the respondent's perception of group homogeneity. However, research findings reported later appear to minimize the problem. We found, for example, that when we used a more objective indicator of class homogeneity in the school, the effects of the class atmosphere were similar to those reported for the peer group.

When we examine the relation between class homogeneity-heterogeneity of peer groups and the political attitudes of working class respondents, we find that homogeneous peer groups function to reinforce working class political norms and existing political cleavages between the working class and other social classes.[23] On the other hand, working class students in heterogeneous class peer groups (hetpeers) appear to be re-socialized in the direction of higher class political

[23] In each case working class students in homogeneous class peer groups assume an attitudinal position which is farther from that of the middle and upper classes than is the attitudinal position of the working class in general.

norms.[24] They are less committed to economic aggrandizement at the expense of political liberty (Gamma: + .37), more disposed toward fulfilling their voting obligation (+ .40), and less intolerant of minority groups (+ .44) than their classmates in homogeneous class peer groups (hompeers).

TABLE 5.4. *Peer Class Environment and Political Orientations among Working Class Students*

	DEPENDENT VARIABLE		
PEER CLASS ENVIRONMENT	STUDENT POLITICIZATION[*]		
	Low (*per cent*)	*Medium* (*per cent*)	*High* (*per cent*)	*N*
Homogeneous	44	26	30	215
Heterogeneous	34	36	30	205

	SYSTEM LEGITIMACY[*]		
	Support (*per cent*)	*Ambivalence* (*per cent*)	*Opposition* (*per cent*)	*N*
Homogeneous	45	42	13	206
Heterogeneous	33	51	16	193

[*] See footnotes 19 and 21 for the items included in these tables.

Peer heterogeneity appears to have no effect upon the development of highly politicized students (Table 5.4). They are found in equal percentages both in homogeneous and heterogeneous peer groups. While the class environment of

[24] The political differences found between working class students in homogeneous and heterogeneous peer groups is explained primarily as a function of the re-socialization process in heterogeneous class peer groups. This difference might also be explained by a process of selection. Heterogeneous peer groups may only select working class members who have the same values as they do or high I.Q. students may select or be co-opted into heterogeneous groups. However, this alternative explanation appears doubtful when the analogous influence of *school* class atmosphere is examined later in this chapter. When using controlled selection, objective criteria of class atmosphere, and the same dependent variables, effects similar to those reported for the peer group middle and upper classes than is the attitudinal position of the working

such intermediary socialization agencies as the peer group adds explanatory power to the movement from low to medium politicization among working class students, other variables must be sought—such as family and peer group politicization —to explain the development of high politicization.

Apparently interaction with higher class peers who tend to be more suspicious of the charismatic tone of Jamaican politics and of alleged political corruption, has a "rationalizing" influence upon working class students. In heterogeneous peer groups they are less supportive and more ambivalent toward the political system than their brethren in homogeneous groups (Table 5.4). This influence of the heterogeneous class peer group upon the legitimacy attitudes of the working class is effective despite the fact that it is contrary to the message in Jamaican "civics" textbooks, which emphasizes support. It suggests that, as in the United States, the informal information the respondent picks up which represents "real" political attitudes is more significant in the socialization process than is his formal education. Wylie makes the same observation regarding informal versus formal political socialization of French school children.[25]

Peer group class environment also has an effect on the economic attitudes of working class students. Students in heterogeneous class peer groups appear to move away from the more liberal positions held by their classmates in homogeneous groups, toward the more conservative economic orientations of the middle and upper classes. They are less inclined to respond that the rich should give up their privileges (+ .48) or that earning limits should be established (+ .37).

Thus we see throughout that heterogeneous class peer groups consistently function to re-socialize the working class toward the level of politicization and political outlook of the higher social classes. On the other hand, the net effect of homogeneous class peer groups is to reinforce the political and economic culture of the working class.

[25] Lawrence Wylie, *Village in the Vaucluse* (New York: Harper, 1964), 2nd ed., pp. 207–09.

School

The school (like the peer group) may reinforce social and political class differences because it is composed of students of the same social class. On the other hand, if students from various classes are assigned to a school, this milieu may promote the re-socialization of working class students by grouping them with adolescents of higher social status.

In her study of selected midwestern schools in the United States, Neugarten found that lower class children and adolescents generally deferred to higher status students in heterogenous class schools by ascribing more favorable personality traits to them than to students of their own class.[26] Other research points out that students from the lower socioeconomic classes who attend heterogeneous class schools have higher educational aspirations than those in more homogeneous schools. The authors attribute the difference in aspirations, at least in part, to the dominant class character of the high school or grade cohort.[27]

[26] Bernice L. Neugarten, "Social Class and Friendship among School Children," *American Sociological Review*, 51 (January, 1946), 305–13.

In her study in Jonesville, Neugarten found students in heterogeneous class environments continued to defer to the perceived "favorable characteristics" of upper class students from elementary school through high school. While in the higher grades in secondary school there was no tendency to defer to lower class students and deference to higher status students was still clearly operative, adolescents were increasingly disposed to defer horizontally in more complex ways. In other words, if one is student council president or captain of the football team this might make him equally, if not more, subject to deference as being from an upper class family. However, as Mary C. Jones has cogently observed, higher social status is strongly associated with access to prestigeous student offices in the high school. Bernice L. Neugarten, "Democracy of Childhood," in William Lloyd Warner, *et al.* (eds.), *Democracy in Jonesville* (New York: Harper, 1949), chap. 5; and Mary C. Jones, "A Study of Socialization Patterns at the High School Level," *Journal of Genetic Psychology*, 93 (September, 1958), 87–111.

[27] Alan B. Wilson, "Residential Segregation of Social Classes and Aspirations of High School Boys," *American Sociological Review*, 24 (December, 1959), 836–45; and John Michael, "High School Climates

In order to test our hypothesis, we ordered the schools in the Caribbean sample by their class environment. Schools categorized as "homogeneous" have a dominant working class environment and, for working class students, are the closest analog to homogeneous class peer groups. The school with the most balanced distribution of classes can be considered the closest analog to the environment of the heterogeneous class peer group.

In determining the class environment of the school, each student is treated as a respondent whose class attributes (objective class of his parents) constitute a part of the total school class climate. This differs from the method used to determine peer class environment. In the latter case, the respondent was used as an informant about the class homogeneity of the peer group.

When we examine the relations between school class climate and the same political variables, a familiar pattern develops. Homogeneous class schools reinforce working class political norms and maintain the political cleavage between the working class and the other social classes. On the other hand, working class students in heterogeneous class schools appear to be re-socialized in the direction of higher class political norms.[28] They are less inclined to forsake political

---

and Plans for Entering College," *Public Opinion Quarterly* 25 (Winter, 1961), 583–95.

[28] It is possible, of course, that differences found between working class students in homogeneous and heterogeneous class schools could be due to selection rather than the operation of different school environments. In other words, working class students with the attitudinal syndrome found among working class students in heterogeneous class schools may actually seek out the more heterogeneous class schools to matriculate. Fortunately, the Jamaican Ministry of Education was able to provide information on this matter. Due to its local school policy, there is no evidence that differences in political attitudes between working class students in homogeneous-heterogeneous class schools is due in any significant degree to selection rather than the socializing influences of the school class environment.

For an expanded discussion of this point see Kenneth P. Langton, *Civic Attitudes of Jamaican High School Students,* Cooperative Research Project, United States Department of Health, Education and Welfare, 1965, p. 198.

liberty for personal gain (Gamma: + .51), more disposed toward fulfilling their voting obligation (+ .38), more tolerant of minority groups (+ .40), more politicized (+ .32), and less supportive and more ambivalent toward the political system than their counterparts in homogeneous schools (+ .30).

School class environment appears to have little effect on economic attitudes. It is possible that among the working class economic attitudes may be more "hard core" and resistant to change than their more esoteric political attitudes. This may be particularly true within the wider school milieu where the pressures to conform and defer to higher class norms may not be as great as in the small face-to-face heterogeneous peer group. The rigidity with which these attitudes are held may vary between cultures. We might find adherence to economic aggrandizement less a part of the working class culture in more affluent societies. This will also depend, of course, on the visibility of class differences in the society.

While this analysis has focused on the maintenance and change of working class values, it would be instructive to review briefly the effect of class heterogeneity on middle and upper class students. Following the same mode of analysis we find that middle class students react to heterogeneous class peer groups in the same way as working class students do. However, the relationships are consistently weaker, particularly on the economic issues. Upper class students with even less reason to defer and with fewer higher status peermates with whom they can interact and identify are least affected by class mixing. In fact, there is no consistent relationship between peer class environment and the political orientations of upper class students. School class environment has no significant effect upon the political orientations of either middle or upper class students.

Thus only among the working class do *both* the peer group and school have an impact. This raises an important question regarding the mutual effects of these two agencies, to which we shall now turn.

Peer Group and School Environment

The interaction between the wider school environment and the socializing process within the peer group poses some intriguing questions. To what degree, for example, has the school class climate outside the peer group contributed to the reported differential influence of peer class environment upon political socialization? Do we still find the reported effect of different peer class environments within schools with relatively homogeneous class milieu?

Does the heterogeneous class environment of both peer group and school have a cumulative effect upon the re-socialization of the working class? Based on previous findings, we might predict that working class hetpeers in heterogeneous class schools will be the farthest removed from the political culture of their class.

In Figure 5.1 we see evidence that the heterogeneous class climate of peer group and school is indeed cumulative. There onment in Peer Groups and Schools among Working Class Students (in per cent)*

FIGURE 5.1. Cumulative Effect of Heterogeneous Class Environment

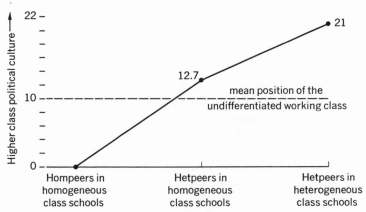

*This figure represents the mean difference between the positions taken by hompeers in homogeneous class schools and hetpeers in homogeneous and heterogeneous class schools on the seven previously discussed variables. The position of hompeers in homogeneous class schools provides the base line.

is a mean change in the predicted direction between the positions taken by hompeers in homogeneous class schools and hetpeers in homogeneous and heterogeneous class schools on all seven of the previously discussed variables. The cumulative direction of change is consistently toward the political culture of the higher classes. The mean difference between the position of hompeers in homogeneous class schools and hetpeers in heterogeneous class schools is 21 per cent.

It is also evident that the impact of the peer group appears to be independent of the broader class environment within the school. When school class homogeneity is controlled, heterogeneous class peer groups still play a significant role in re-socializing working class students in the direction of higher class political norms.

Finally, it seems obvious that to compare the political culture of an undifferentiated working class with that of higher classes tends to underestimate the political cleavages in the society, because the cleavage between the political culture of hompeers in homogeneous class schools and the higher classes is much greater.[29] It also seems likely that this differentiation will increase as the respondents pass into the early years of adulthood.

School Class Climate and the Political Socialization Process in the United States

Other than the suggestive literature discussed above, there appear to be no empirical studies of the effects of peer group or school class climate on the political socialization process in the United States. In 1964, however, a study was conducted in Detroit, Michigan, of school children's reaction to the assassination of President Kennedy. Data from this sample of 1349 students may illuminate the potential influence of the social class milieu in the American school upon politically

[29] The mean difference between the positions taken by the undifferentiated working class and working class hompeers in homogeneous class schools on the seven variables is 10 per cent, with the latter group consistently taking a position farthest removed from that of the higher classes.

relevant variables. Two questions in the survey asked what the children thought about the denial of Lee Harvey Oswald's civil rights, another attempted to ascertain their idealization of American Presidents. An analysis of the data reveals an inverse correlation between social class and the propensity to deny Oswald his civil rights (Gamma: − .40, − .44).[30] Lower class Jamaicans were quick to deny basic civil rights. Working class students in America are also more likely than the middle or upper class students to be "glad" that President Kennedy's alleged assassin was killed by Jack Ruby, and to want to see the President's murderer "shot or beat up." By the same token, as the strongest support for the political system is found among the lower classes in the Caribbean, students from the working class in the United States are also more likely to idealize the role of President and to feel that all American Presidents have "done their job well" than are middle or upper class students (+ .38). At the elementary level, the tendency for working class students to be more deferential toward political authority and leadership was underscored by Greenstein's study in New Haven and Hess and Torney's national study.[31]

To examine the impact of school class environment upon these attitudes among working class students, the schools in the Detroit study were ordered by their objective class environment as were the schools in the Caribbean study.[32]

When we examine the relations between school class climate and these three variables in Detroit, we find a consistent pattern. Heterogeneous class schools appear to be resocializing working class students in the direction of higher class political norms: Working class students in heterogeneous class schools are less inclined to deny Oswald his civil

[30] The respondents' social class is based on their fathers' occupations.

[31] Greenstein, *Children and Politics*, pp. 101–02; and Hess and Torney, *The Development of Political Attitudes in Children*, pp. 135–36.

[32] Because of the reduced N resulting from the class control, it was necessary to include both primary and secondary schools in the index (i.e., grades 4, 6, 8, 10, 12). This may diminish the reported effect of school class climate to the extent that status consciousness is a corollary of the maturation process. See Harvey and Rutherford, "Status in the Informal Group."

rights (+ .44, + .37) than are those in more homogeneous environments. Interestingly enough, they also take a less benevolent view of the presidency (+ .36)—a finding not incompatible with the greater political cynicism found among working class Jamaicans in heterogeneous class schools.

Conclusion

We have seen that working class students in heterogeneous class schools and peer groups consistently differ in the same direction from their counterparts in homogeneous class environments. If, as seems to be the case, peer groups and the class milieu of schools are important agencies of change, then the question many educators and students of politics may ask is: How can we take advantage of students' potentialities for change—and of the power of peer and school environment to induce change—in such ways that change will most probably occur in the direction of our educational, social, and political objectives?

The social scientist would suggest, on the basis of the preceding findings, that there is a potential for introducing "modernizing" norms to the lower classes by way of heterogeneous class environments. He might also point out that the organization of vocational and technical schools for the working class, as is being done in many less industrialized countries, may reinforce existent political-culture cleavages within the society. However, the results of this study indicate that any manipulation of peer grouping or class environment within schools should be preceded by a careful survey of one's objectives and an analysis of the political culture of the different social classes. For we found that working class students in a heterogeneous class climate (Caribbean) not only are more politicized, have more "democratic" attitudes, give greater support to civil liberties, and have more positive orientations toward voting, they are also more economically conservative. Equally, if not more important, in a culture where the higher classes tend to be more politically alienated (Jamaica), working class students in heterogeneous class environments are more ambivalent and less supportive of the political system than are those in more homogeneous class climates.

This means that the existence of potential system "pathologies" in the form of political class cleavages may be less threatening to long-run stability than the re-socializing effect of heterogeneous class school and peer environments. While this process may reduce class cleavages, it creates an enlarged category of students who are not only more politicized but also less supportive of the political system—certainly a potentially critical output in national political systems in their early stages of development.

However, the problems which the socializing function of different peer group and school environments may create for the political system does not mean that the planner must seek to enable the lower classes to live comfortably with their "inferior" social and cultural status, à la Huxley. What it does mean is that the creation of heterogeneous class socializing environments to promote the stability of democratic political systems will be maximized when the higher classes are generally supportive of the political system.

CHAPTER SIX

INFLUENCE OF DIFFERENT AGENCIES IN POLITICAL SOCIALIZATION

Kenneth P. Langton and David A. Karns

▌▌▌▌▌ In Chapter 1 we saw that an increasing amount of research is devoted to the respective roles of the family, school, and peer group in the political socialization process. This research, however, has mainly confined itself to the analysis of single agencies. We have generally avoided the larger question of the *relative* importance of each of these agencies. Attempts to map the political development of individuals must inevitably become involved with the relative contribution of different social institutions throughout the life cycle. This question, as much as any other, represents the substantive and methodological frontier of political socialization research.

While little research has focused on the differential effect of these social institutions, two contemporary studies have drawn significant conclusions regarding the relative influence of various agencies in political socialization. First is the important investigation of American elementary school children by Hess and Torney, who view the school as "the most important and effective" agent of political socialization in the United States.[1] While this may indeed be the case for elementary school children, their main source of evidence

---

This chapter is a revision by Kenneth P. Langton of an article by Kenneth P. Langton and David A. Karns, "The Relative Influence of the Family Peer Group and School in the Development of Political Efficacy," *Western Political Quarterly*, Spring, 1969.

[1] Hess and Torney, *The Development of Political Attitudes in Children*, pp. 101–15.

is a series of quasi-longitudinal developmental plots. Without controls for school characteristics it is difficult to know if the school actually has some measurable political impact or if we are viewing natural developmental rates affected by stimuli primarily from sources outside the school. Moreover, assertions regarding the relative impact of the family and school would be more convincing if their differential effects were viewed within the same causal model.

Almond and Verba pioneered an attempt to view the relative effect of participatory environments in three different agencies on the socialization of political competence. They concluded from their five-nation study that the work group was most influential followed by the school and family.[2] However the major table they present as evidence of cumulative effects (p. 367) was derived from a series of contingency tables in which the impact of one agent on high competence was analyzed while controlling for the participatory environment in *one* of the other two agencies. But this provides little support for their major generalization regarding *relative* impact. If this hypothesis was tested using a single model which viewed the independent effect of each agent, it is possible that it might be confirmed. Of course, the opposite is also possible.

Another problem given little consideration in the socialization literature is that the influence of an agency may be concentrated within a particular level or stage of a child's development. That is, the family or school could play an important role in moving children from low-to-medium political efficacy, whereas the peer group's influence is concentrated in the medium-to-high efficacy range.

To gain insight into both problems we use a causal modeling technique (1) to estimate the relative role of the family, peer group, and school in the development of political efficacy, and (2) to determine how the different agencies affect each level of the dependent variable. While these questions are of sufficient theoretical interest to be amenable to empirical testing in any political culture in which the agencies

[2] Almond and Verba, *The Civic Culture*, chap. 12.

exist, the primary source of data for this analysis is the Caribbean sample.

Political Efficacy

The literature on political efficacy and its correlates is voluminous.[3] An individual's belief that he can effectively participate in politics and in this way he has some control over the action of political decision-makers has important consequences for the political system. A feeling of political efficacy correlates with increased voting and political participation, organizational membership, positive attitudes toward the legitimacy of the political system, and a number of other politically relevant dependent variables.

A belief in personal political efficacy has many roots. An individual may base his estimate of his capacity to influence governmental policy on his direct experience with government or its agencies, or he might base it on more indirect evidence. Children begin at an early age to develop a sense of their own capacity to manage the world around them.[4] In time some develop a self-confident, positive attitude toward the emergent problems of political life, while others see themselves giving way to the political environment, unable to manage the complex political forces they encounter. Some individuals project their early status in the family to the political arena, others observe their parents attempting to be politically influential and learn from their experiences, still others base their personal estimate on what they hear about how much the "common man" can influence politics. No doubt many if not all of these factors enter into the de-

---

[3] Almond and Verba, *ibid;* Angus Campbell, *et al., The American Voter;* Lester Milbrath, *Political Participation* (Chicago: Rand McNally, 1965); and Herbert McClosky and John H. Schaar, "Psychological Dimensions of Anomy," *American Sociological Review,* 30 (February, 1965), 14–40. For additional bibliography on political efficacy see David Easton and Jack Dennis, "The Child's Acquisition of Regime Norms: Political Efficacy," *American Political Science Review,* 61 (March, 1967), 25–38.

[4] Easton and Dennis, "The Child's Acquisition of Regime Norms."

velopment of political efficacy, although some may be more important at different stages in the life cycle.

We hypothesize that the development of an individual's sense of political efficacy is explained in large part by the degree of politicization within the groups or social institutions in which he participates. Individuals who are raised or who participate in group or school environments where the general atmosphere is highly politicized will be more likely to develop the view that politics is amenable to their personal influence, i.e., they will feel more politically efficacious.

In the family, for example, this may come about through the child's internalization of the politicized parental role, or by a more indirect means. In the latter case the politicized group environment may inspire a process which translates ego strength into political efficacy, i.e., it makes ego politically relevant.[5] Even though we could not measure the ego strength of our respondents, we were able to determine their sense of political efficacy and the level of politicization in each of the agencies concerned.[6] The following discussion

[5] A preliminary analysis of election data collected by the Survey Research Center, University of Michigan, indicated the following general relations between ego strength, family politicization, and political efficacy.

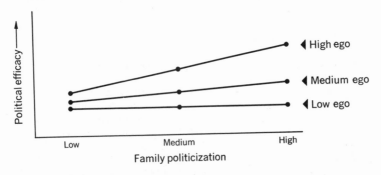

[6] The following items were combined into a Guttman-type political efficacy scale with a CR of .93.
  1. When people like me become adults we will not have any influence on what government does.

will proceed from a simple bivariate examination of the relationships to a more comprehensive causal analysis.

Socialization Agencies

One generalization we can make from examining the tables is that the relations between family, peer group, and school politicization on one hand, and political efficacy, on the other, are not linear.

As might be expected, children reared in families in which parents are interested in politics, discuss politics among themselves, and also participate in political activities are more likely to develop a sense of political efficacy than are those students from less politicized families.[7] Table 6.1 indicates that the level of family politicization is an important factor in moving children from low-to-medium efficacy, but apparently has less effect in moving students into the high efficacy category.[8]

To investigate the politicization-political efficacy hypothesis within the peer group, these groups were arrayed on a politicization continuum based on the amount of political discussion within the peer group.[9]

---

    2. The political views and activities of students are very important.

    3. Sometimes politics and government seem so complicated that a person like me can't really understand what is going on.

[7] The family politicization index is based on the following questions:

    1. How interested would you say your parents have been in politics?

    2. How often have your parents discussed politics?

    3. How often have your parents participated in political activities (attended election meetings, talked to politicians and so forth)?

[8] If the family's influence extended significantly to high efficacy, the percentage of highly efficacious students in the more politicized families in Table 1 should be greater than 12 per cent. There is a sufficient number of these students in the sample (141) so that theoretically the percentage could go to 100 per cent.

[9] Respondents were asked how often they discussed politics with their best school friends. The response categories were "often," "sometimes," or "never." Students who answered "often" were considered members of the most highly politicized peer groups, those who an-

TABLE 6.1. *Family Politicization and Students' Sense of Political Efficacy*

FAMILY POLITICIZATION	STUDENTS' SENSE OF POLITICAL EFFICACY			
	Low (*per cent*)	Medium (*per cent*)	High (*per cent*)	N
Low	36	56	8	317
Medium	22	66	12	608
High	13	75	12	82

Those respondents in the least politicized peer groups, i.e., those in which they and their friends "never" discuss politics, are the most likely to have a low sense of political efficacy (Table 6.2). There is an increase in efficacy as we move from the least to the most politicized peer groups.

It is possible that some of the differences found in Table 6.2 are due to selection. In other words, the more politicized peer groups attract the more efficacious students. We are aware of this problem, and that it can be explored best with a longitudinal design. However, we did examine the relations between grade level and efficacy for each level of peer politicization.

TABLE 6.2. *Peer Group Politicization and Student Members' Sense of Political Efficacy*

PEER GROUP POLITICIZATION	STUDENTS' SENSE OF POLITICAL EFFICACY			
	Low (*per cent*)	Medium (*per cent*)	High (*per cent*)	N
Low	40	52	8	316
Medium	24	66	10	656
High	18	66	16	171

swered "never" were considered members in the least politicized peer groups.

The secondary schools have five grades running from eighth to twelfth. Approximately the same percentage of eighth-grade students from highly politicized peer groups are low in efficacy as are those from peer groups with a low level of politicization (38 and 39 per cent, respectively). This suggests that during the first year of high school the more politicized peer groups are not recruiting only efficacious members, and that unless these peer groups are highly unstable—and there is no evidence that this is the case—differences in political efficacy found between groups at different levels of politicization are due to the socializing effects of group political environment after the student enters high school.

A school that allows political debate and discussion should also have an effect on the development of political efficacy. To explore the more formal political atmosphere in the schools, respondents were asked how often they discussed and debated political and social issues in their respective schools. On the basis of their answers the schools were ordered by their degree of politicization. In this ordering the schools tended to cluster at two points thereby creating a dichotomous independent variable.

TABLE 6.3. *School Politicization and Students' Sense of Political Efficacy*

SCHOOL POLITICIZATION	STUDENTS' SENSE OF POLITICAL EFFICACY			
	Low (per cent)	Medium (per cent)	High (per cent)	N
Low	35	54	11	823
High	20	71	9	464

Table 6.3 reports the relations between school politicization and political efficacy. Within the school, as in the family and peer group, there is a relation between respondents' participation in a politicized institutional atmosphere and their sense of political efficacy. Again, however, the relation-

ship between the two variables is not linear. The impact of the school is primarily at the low-and-medium levels of efficacy.

There are a number of standard means for summarizing and reporting the three relationships just examined. We could report the correlations. However, reporting only a gamma correlation for Table 6.1 (.29), for example, would not be a very adequate summary of the relationship as it reflects the lack of monotonicity, and would mask the movement we found from low-to-medium efficacy. The bivariate table, on the other hand, tells us nothing about possible complementary effects of the other two agencies. For example, is the movement from low-to-medium efficacy in Table 6.1 wholly the result of family politicization, or is it due in part to the effect of peer group and school politicization? Conversely, do these two agencies mask the influence of family politicization upon the movement from medium-to-high efficacy? The answers clearly call for some type of multivariate analysis.

Relative Influence of
Family, Peer Group, and School

It is not unusual to regard non-linear relationships such as those found in Tables 6.1–3 as lacking statistical and substantive importance when measured by instruments which assume linearity. The expectation (often implicit) is that the independent variable should affect the full range of the dependent. In other words, changes in the level of politicization of the family should affect both the movement from low-to-medium and from medium-to-high efficacy. However, there is no reason to assume that moving a person from medium-to-high efficacy is qualitatively the same, or as "easy," as moving him from low-to-medium. In many cases the family may have reached the zenith of its influence when its children have developed a medium level of political efficacy. The movement from medium-to-high may have to await the later additive effect of secondary socialization agencies.

We have few answers for these types of questions. Between what ranges of political efficacy do family, peer group, and school have their greatest influence? How do they differ in this respect? Is there some type of independent factor or agency which plays a particularly important role in moving an individual into the highest reaches of a politically significant dimension?

Clearly, a relationship should be judged by what it tells us about the role of a given agency in the political socialization process. Whether it is linear or not is significant information but this should not necessarily provide the only criteria for determining its substantive or statistical importance. Actually the lack of linearity may be one of the first indications that we should continue to probe the relationship to understand better the limits of the socialization agency's influence along a given political dimension.

This discussion suggests that an appropriate analytical scheme for our data would estimate the relative effects of *each level* of the independent variable upon the movement into *each level* of the dependent variable (Figure 6.1). As family, peer group, and school all appear to have an effect on political efficacy, the larger question of the relative independent influence of each agency (as well as each of its categories) should be incorporated into the same model. This calls for some mode of causal analysis.

FIGURE 6.1.   A Model To Be Tested

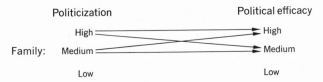

Blalock, Simon, and Wright describe the most popular forms of causal modeling.[10] There are disciplinary and ana-

10 Herbert Blalock, Jr., *Causal Inferences in Non-Experimental Research* (Chapel Hill: University of North Carolina Press, 1964); Herbert Simon, "Causal Ordering and Identifiability," in W. C. Hood and T. C. Koopmans, *Studies in Econometric Method* (New York: Wiley, 1953),

lytical differences between these authors' works, but all are based on the product moment correlation coefficient. Our first inclination was to use these correlations and regression techniques to construct a causal model of the socialization process. However, the computation of the product moment correlation assumes a linear relation between the two variables. This was not the case with the family, peer group, or school.[11]

In our search for an appropriate analytical scheme we also rejected probit analysis as a possible technique because it assumes linear, continuous independent variables and a dichotomized dependent variable.[12] Our dependent variable, political efficacy, is trichotomous. Table 6.1 suggests there is a significant difference between the medium and high levels of efficacy. Dichotomizing the variable by collapsing the medium and high categories into one would therefore obscure important features of the political culture and socialization process such as (1) the incidence of high political efficacy, and (2) the ability of socialization agencies to develop a high sense of efficacy among the citizenry—information which may be particularly significant in less developed polities.

The analytical technique we selected was a causal analysis procedure, designed by James S. Coleman, which uses only the discrete ordinal categorization of both the dependent

---

pp. 49–74; S. Wright, "The Interpretation of Multivariate Systems," in O. Kempthorne, et al., Statistics and Mathematics in Biology (Ames: Iowa State College Press, 1954), pp. 11–33.

[11] The lack of linearity makes product moment correlations inappropriate, for the attenuating effect of applying such correlations to non-linear relationships is well known. In our three basic tables the largest product moment correlation was .31. The magnitude of these correlations reflects the general findings in much of the political socialization literature as well as other political studies. If non-linearity existed in these other studies and served to attenuate the magnitude of the correlations, a model whose base correlations do not reflect linearity-non-linearity might have been more appropriate.

[12] D. Finey, Probit Analysis (Cambridge: Cambridge University Press, 1952).

and independent variables and assumes that the effect of the agents are additive.[13]

The result of the analysis is a set of "causal coefficients" which summarizes the causal influence of each level of the independent variable as it affects each level of the dependent variable. Coleman's technique, as adapted for a trichotomous dependent variable, will be used to assess the relative importance of the politicized peer group, school, and family in the socialization of political efficacy.

For a complete discussion of the derivation of Coleman's causal technique, the reader should consult the original source. Only the general principles and some methodological detail will be outlined here and this will be done essentially in the footnotes.[14] Therefore the reader who wants to may move directly to the next section, which presents the findings using the causal analysis.

[13] James S. Coleman, *Introduction to Mathematical Sociology* (Glencoe: Free Press, 1964), chap. 4.

[14] For explanatory purposes we shall assume that a dependent variable has two states, HD and LD, and that the independent variable has states HI and LI. Next assume that a perfect causal relationship exists between the two variables. We should then expect that in figure A only cells n_1 and n_4 would have data.

FIGURE A

	LD	HD
LI	n_1	n_2
HI	n_3	n_4

In a set of actual empirical data, it is likely that the two off-diagonal cells would not be empty. Assuming a two-variable isolated system, the off-diagonal entries would be attributed to the effects of random shocks. Causally, in figure A, there are two major factors affecting the size of n_1 and n_4 and one factor affecting the size of n_2 and n_3. The size of n_4 is determined by possessing HD and random shock upward (e_2). By random shock upward we mean all those other factors that may cause an individual to be HD other than HI. The size of n_2 is determined solely by random shock upwards (downwards in the case of n_3), in other words, all those factors not related to I.

A final assumption is that the system of causal effects is at equilibrium. This assumption is not necessary to the procedure, but if the system is not at equilibrium, then the deviation from the state must be specified. There is an equilibrium when the number of individuals moving from HD to LD due to random shock is equal to those moving from LD to HD. For simplicity, and in accordance with standard causal modeling assumptions, we shall assume equilibrium throughout our discussion.

At equilibrium, n_1 is the result of e_1, the shock downward plus the lack of HI or a. Therefore n_1 can be characterized by the quantity $e_1 + a$; n_2 is the result of e_2 only; n_3 is characterized by e_1 and n_4 by $e_2 + a$. Figure B graphically presents these characterizations where HD is above the horizontal line, LD below the horizontal line, LI to the left of the vertical and HI to the right. The quantities e_1, e_2, and a are then obtained by the method of least squares. In this simple case, a equals the differences between the percentages in HI and LI. Exactly the same procedure can be followed when the dependent variable is dichotomous and there are several independent variables. Each combination of independent variable categories is assigned an expression of its causal effects and the best approximations for the values of the causal coefficients are computed by the method of least squares. In figure B_2, the causal combination producing HD with HI_A and HI_B is $e_2 + a + b$, i.e., the effects are *additive*. Figure B_3 depicts how Coleman suggests treating a trichotomized independent variable. The effect of having a medium amount of I_A is a; the additional effect of being high on I_A is .a so that the total effect of being high on I_A and high on I_B is now $e_2 + a + .a + b$.

The same idea carries through to the case of a trichotomized dependent variable and a dichotomized independent variable depicted in figure B_4 with the addition that a refers to the causal effect between LD and MD and b to the effect between MD and HD.

An expression P{H/12} should be read the percentage of a sample as defined by two characteristics that is high in efficacy. If 1 stands for medium family politicization and 2 for high school politicization, P is that highly efficacious portion of the sample characterized by both medium family and high school politicization. Likewise, P{H/12} − P{H/1} compares the percentage of high efficacy in two subsamples which both have medium family politicization but differ on school politicization since one has a high and the other has a low level of school politicization.

The general solutions for a and b using the same conventions are:

$$a_i = \frac{1}{k} \sum_j (P\{L/i\} - P\{L/ij\})$$

$$b_i = \frac{1}{k} \sum_j (P\{H/ij\} - P\{H/j\})$$

The symbol i refers to the independent variables, if dichotomized, or

FIGURE B₁

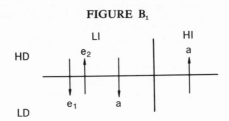

FIGURE B₂

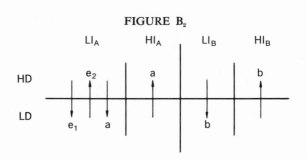

FIGURE B₃

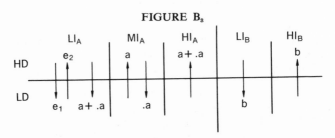

FIGURE B₄

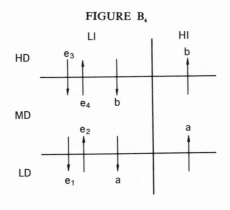

the independent variables in all states if polychotomous. k is the number of comparisons which are contained within the summation over j. j, the index on the summation symbol, refers to the states of the other independent variables, other than variable i, which are causally related to the dependent variable.

If we have three dichotomous independent variables (1, 2, and 3) and we note their presence by an integer and absence by 0, $P\{H/120\}$ is the probability of being in the high state of the dependent variable given the presence of variables 1 and 2 but not 3. The set of equations expanded for a_i which are derived from the general trichotomous dependent variable is:

$$a_1 = \tfrac{1}{4} \left[(P\{L/000\} - P\{L/100\}) + (P\{L/003\} - P\{L/103\}) \right.$$
$$\left. + (P\{L/020\} - P\{L/120\}) + (P\{L/023\} - P\{L/123\}) \right]$$

$$a_2 = \tfrac{1}{4} \left[(P\{L/000\} - P\{L/020\}) + (P\{L/003\} - P\{L/023\}) \right.$$
$$\left. + (P\{L/100\} - P\{L/120\}) + (P\{L/103\} - P\{L/123\}) \right]$$

$$a_3 = \tfrac{1}{4} \left[(P\{L/000\} - P\{L/003\}) + (P\{L/100\} - P\{L/103\}) \right.$$
$$\left. + (P\{L/020\} - P\{L/023\}) + (P\{L/120\} - P\{L/123\}) \right]$$

$$b_1 = \tfrac{1}{4} \left[(P\{H/100\} - P\{H/000\}) + (P\{H/120\} - P\{H/020\}) \right.$$
$$\left. + (P\{H/103\} - P\{H/003\}) + (P\{H/123\} - P\{H/023\}) \right]$$

$$b_2 = \tfrac{1}{4} \left[(P\{H/020\} - P\{H/000\}) + (P\{H/120\} - P\{H/100\}) \right.$$
$$\left. + (P\{H/023\} - P\{H/003\}) + (P\{H/123\} - P\{H/103\}) \right]$$

$$b_3 = \tfrac{1}{4} \left[(P\{H/003\} - P\{H/000\}) + (P\{H/103\} - P\{H/100\}) \right.$$
$$\left. + (P\{H/023\} - P\{H/020\}) + (P\{H/123\} - P\{H/120\}) \right]$$

The random shocks cannot be neatly summarized in a simple general equation, but in this case the random shock from medium to low is:

$$e_1 = \tfrac{1}{8} \left[3P\{L/123\} + 2(P\{L/100\} - P\{L/000\}) - P\{L/100\} \right.$$
$$\left. + P\{L/103\} + P\{L/120\} \right]$$

In Table 6.3, the conditional percentages of being in the high state of efficacy given individuals in the low and high states of school politicization were 11.0 and 9.0 respectively. The implication which may be drawn is that increasing school politicization is accompanied by decreasing efficacy. The empirical result can be explained through further analysis, but violates, as it stands, our second theoretical assumption. Mathematics does not know very much about socialization theory, and merely assigns whatever values give the best fitting solution without further thought. Since this case could yield a negative causal coefficient (as could other cases with wide variances in cell frequencies), we were confronted with the problem of interpreting the negative coefficient in the light of our

Findings

Figure 6.2 presents the relative effect of family, peer group, and school politicization upon the development of political efficacy. An arrow in this figure indicates a causal relationship greater than zero. The number in parenthesis affixed to each arrow is the causal coefficient. This is not a correlation coefficient nor any variant of it. Instead, the causal coefficient indicates the percentage of the sample that will have a given level of efficacy (medium or high) as a result of being subjected to a particular environment in one of the

---

theoretical assumption. If the negative value is truly a mathematical artifact, other coefficients should not change appreciably when the state yielding the negative result is omitted, that is, if a_2 is negative, a_1, $a_{.1}$, a_3 should not change much if a_2 is removed as a relevant cause. Rather than having two dichotomous and one trichotomous independent variables, we would only have one dichotomous and one trichotomous. One general procedure was that when the computation yielded a negative coefficient, we assumed that the independent variable or state did not have a causal influence. Parenthetically, all negative values were very close to zero and their removal produced no significant changes in the other coefficients.

We also had to confront a credibility gap. What significance can be ascribed to coefficients derived from percentages based on sub-samples of six as compared to subsamples of 40? The problem, which is not unique to this study, can be confronted in two ways. First, categories could be collapsed until most cells contain enough cases for reasonably stable calculations of percentages. We chose not to follow this course because the original examination of the data indicates that there are subtle differences in the effects of categories which would be collapsed. Therefore we followed a semi-Bayesian approach in which cell entries are weighted by a function of the size of the cell entry in such a way that the larger the entry the more confidence assigned to percentages based on that entry. The function has to be always positive and asymptotically approach 1 as n becomes large. Specifically, we used the weighting factor $n/(n + 2)$ where n is the total number of persons with a given combination of independent categories. We plotted this weighting function for various n. The comparable value of $n/(n + 1)$ was also plotted. The effect of choosing one or the other appears to be inconsequential except at very small n. The results of a test run using both functions yielded differences ranging from 0.001 to 0.004. The particular function does not appear to have distorted the results of our analysis and it did allow us to maintain the same fineness which was present in the survey results.

FIGURE 6.2. Relative Influence of Family, Peer Group, and School on Political Efficacy

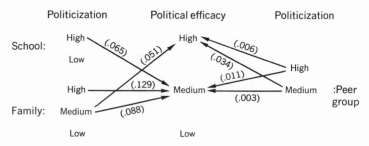

socialization agencies, holding constant the effect of the other two agencies.[15] For example, a coefficient of .065 equals 6.5 per cent. This coefficient is somewhat analogous to the result obtained from squaring a correlation coefficient to detemine the percentage of variance explained.

The additive effect of the politicized environment in the three socialization agencies (Figure 6.2) accounts for the placement of 39 per cent of the sample in the medium-and-high levels of political efficacy, or 51 per cent of all the students who are in the medium-and-high efficacy range. This explains the efficacy level of a sizeable portion of the sample, considering that we are only looking at one aspect of the socialization agency—its level of politicization—and at only three of the many agencies that may influence the development of political efficacy.

Of the three agencies the family has the greatest impact on the development of political efficacy. Its combined effect accounts for the efficacy level of 27 per cent of the sample[16] (or 36 per cent of the students in medium-and-high efficacy ranges) in contrast to 5.4 and 6.5 per cent for the peer group and school, respectively. The family not only has the great-

[15] This is analogous in a multivariate sense with a quasi-experimental procedure of grouping a population on different states of an independent variable and comparing the differences in conditional probabilities of achieving given states of a dependent variable.

[16] One would have to square a standard correlation coefficient of .52 to explain this amount of variance.

est absolute influence (21.7 per cent) on the movement from low-to-medium efficacy, but it also plays a greater role (5.1 per cent) at the high efficacy level. Only 11.1 per cent of the total sample scored high on the efficacy scale, and the politicized atmosphere of the family accounts for the placement of 45 per cent of this group.[17]

The impact of the school is confined to the medium efficacy range (6.5 per cent) where its influence is overshadowed by that of the family. The effect of the peer group, on the other hand, is contained almost exclusively in the movement from medium-to-high efficacy. The peer group accounts for the placement of 4 per cent of the sample at the high efficacy level or 37 per cent of all the students who scored high in political efficacy.

Because the influence of these socialization agencies may be affected by class background, we repeated the analysis reported in Figure 6.2 but this time controlling for the social class of the respondents.[18] The family continues to play a dominant role in each social class, although among upper class students its total effect (16.7 per cent) relative to that of the peer group (5.4 per cent) and school (13.8 per cent) is less than it was among the lower classes (Figure 6.3). Its influence on the movement from low-to-medium efficacy is predominant across the three social classes, although it diminishes relative to that of the school among the upper class. There is a similar pattern in the movement from medium-to-high efficacy—the family has proportionately greater influence among the lower classes but is overtaken

[17] Secondary school students in the Caribbean, as in most under-industrialized countries, are an elite group. For example, in Jamaica less than 10 percent of the secondary-school-age population attends the government-aided high schools. While the combined socialization environment has been sufficiently strong to move a majority of the students into the medium efficacy range (65 percent), it has provided only a small corps of students with a high sense of efficacy. In this context, those agencies moving students from medium-to-high efficacy take on added significance.

[18] As previously, the respondent's social class is based upon his parent's occupation and education.

FIGURE 6.3. Relative Influence of Family, Peer Group, and School on Political Efficacy, by Social Class

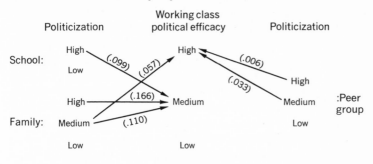

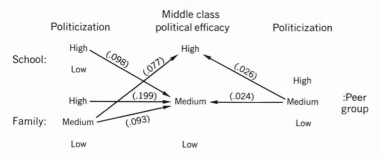

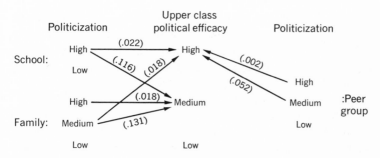

in the upper class, and for the first time, surpassed by the influence of the peer group.

The school is more effective than the peer group across all social classes in moving students from low-to-medium efficacy. Its maximum influence is among upper class students (11.6 per cent). The larger effect of the school is somewhat surprising, since we expected a small face-to-face group, such as the peer group, to be more influential than the broader school environment. In this regard it is interesting that the effect of the school tends to be almost solely at the medium range of the efficacy scale, whereas the peer group focuses almost exclusively, across all social classes, on moving students who already have a medium sense of efficacy into the high range. To the extent this is a qualitatively more difficult move than from low-to-medium, we might rightly expect a more intimate face-to-face group such as the peer group (or family) to have the greater influence.

While the causal analysis underscores the relative influence of the different agencies, it also indicates that much of the peer group influence on the low-to-medium efficacy range reported in the bivariate analysis was due to interaction effects with the family and school. At the same time, the simple bivariate analysis underestimated the relative influence of the family in moving students from medium-to-high efficacy.

Summary and Conclusion

When we first examined the relations between a politicized family, peer group, or school, and the development of political efficacy among secondary school students, we found each agency had some influence on the development of efficacy. However, this type of analysis told us nothing about the *relative* influence of these agencies.

Since the lack of linear relationships raised important substantive questions concerning the role of socialization agencies, we selected a causal modeling technique that would not only estimate the relative role of the agencies but also would tell us how the independent variable affected *each level* of the dependent variable.

The family accounted for almost four times more movement along the entire efficacy scale than either peer group or school. In fact, it was the only agency that moved students along the entire range of the efficacy scale. The family also exceeded significantly the other two agencies in creating a medium level of efficacy, although this relative influence was reduced among the upper classes. The same pattern was visible at the high efficacy range. Among working and middle classes the politicized family accounted for the placement of more highly efficacious respondents than either peer group or school. But among the upper class the family succumbed to the dominant influence of the peer group.

Upper classes appear to be less subject to the influence of the family. As studies in other cultures have indicated, they may be relatively more affected by class-bound cultural cues from outside the family—cues which are more readily transmitted through the informal school and peer environment.

Additional increments of family politicization beyond the medium politicization level had relatively little effect in either of the classes in creating a high sense of efficacy. Apparently there is a threshold of family politicization beyond which additional increments have little influence.

Although the family influences movement along the entire efficacy dimension, the peer group and school operate at different ends of this scale. The broader, less intimate school environment moves students from low-to-medium efficacy but has almost no influence at the high efficacy range. The face-to-face peer group, on the other hand, concentrates almost exclusively on what may be a more difficult socialization task—moving students from medium-to-high political efficacy.

Because of restricted entry into the secondary school system, high school students in the Caribbean, like those in other less-industrialized countries, are an elite group. We saw that the total socialization environment was sufficiently strong to move a majority of these students into the medium efficacy range. An important part of this process involved the politicized environment of the family (33 per cent) and school (10 per cent) which together accounted for the placement of 43 per cent of those at the medium level.

However, the socialization process as a whole proved less

effective at the upper efficacy range. It was able to provide only a small corps of adolescents with a high sense of efficacy. In this context, the findings take on added significance, since the politicized family (45 per cent) and peer group (37 per cent) account for the placement of 82 per cent of all students found at the higher level. Clearly the incidence of family and peer group politicization has an important bearing on the national distribution of high efficacy.

This study suggests the inadequacy of single-agency analysis of the socialization process which ignores the larger question of *relative influence*. Not only does the latter allow a more comprehensive mapping of the political development of individuals, but it reduces the likelihood of undiscovered complementary and interactive effects with other agencies. The establishment of relative influence rankings, however, does not complete the task. Future socialization models must contend not only with the relative importance of agents but also with their differential influence within selected ranges of the dimensions under investigation. There is some reason to believe that the truncated role of the different agents found in this study, if not precisely duplicated in other cultures, may be descriptive of a general phenomenon which permeates the entire socialization process.

CHAPTER SEVEN

SUMMARY AND CONCLUSIONS

IIIIII This study examined the role played by selected social agencies in the political socialization process. Chapter 1 was introductory. Our analysis of the political socialization of Jamaican and American secondary school students was an effort to add empirical substance to some of the general questions raised and to provide, when the data allowed, a cross-national base for our generalizations.

Although both national samples are of adolescents in secondary schools, the analysis potentially reflects on a broader span of the life cycle, particularly as inter-generational relations are examined and the quasi-longitudinal nature of the Caribbean sample is exploited. Moreover, high school students in both the Caribbean and the United States, as is probably true generally, are at a significant point in their maturation. They are nearly ready to leave their parents' family. They are also approaching the end of high school which for most means the termination of formal civics education. For the most part, they have not yet married or begun an occupation, both of which will create new patterns of influence. Therefore, they are at an important stage in which to assess the influence of present and past political socialization agencies.

Among the different agents that may have some impact upon political learning, we selected three which are generally assumed to be of prime importance: family, school, and peer group. Each has multiple facets and can be studied from many different perspectives. Within the family we examined (1) the political relevance of family power structure and (2) the relative influence of mother and father in transmitting political orientations to their children. At the secondary level, the focus is on the school and role of the formal civics curriculum. Since we believe that important political learning takes place within the less formal milieu of school and peer group, the impact of this environment is also scrutinized. The choice of perspectives at each agent level was dictated by a set of theoretically compelling questions, capable of being tested in different cultures and relatively neglected by existing empirical literature on political socialization. In this sense the study is less a synthesis of this literature than, hopefully, a contribution to it.

As the child moves through the family, peer group, school, and the host of adult institutions to which he will be exposed, and as his path of political learning is more clearly traced, the question of the relative impact of these agents ultimately arises. In the final part, we sought to integrate some of the earlier concerns with individual agencies by incorporating the three institutions into a single causal model to demonstrate their relative impact upon selected political orientations.

Before proceeding further, a few points of caution must be stressed. First, to answer the question: "How do people learn politically relevant attitudes and behavior patterns?," we have focused on the agencies in which the socialization process takes place. While the nature of this process, whether it best be explained in terms of learning, role, personality theory, and so forth, is discussed in Chapter 1 and touched on throughout the study, the basic evidence consists of relationships (or their absence) drawn between certain characteristics of the agents and the political orientations of the adolescents. That this choice of emphasis is a general problem in socialization research is to state the obvious. More to the point is that these patterned relationships provide the first link in a chain of circumstantial evidence which calls for explication, possibly in terms of such processes as "learning" which, in the past, have been less central to the concern of political scientists.

Another question relates to the perspective from which the socialization process is viewed. Do we stress the role of the socializer or the role of the learner? Terms such as "teaching," "training," "inculcation," "transmission," and even "socialization" seem to suggest that the initiative lies with the agent. On the other hand, words like "acquisition," "internalization," learning," and "adaptation" suggest a model in which the member, himself, plays an active role.[1] Although a combination of both models is undoubtedly necessary for a comprehensive explanation, the major emphasis in most socialization research is, either explicitly or implicitly, on the agent-initiator.

In this study, the stress has been on the role of the agent. The socialization process, however, is recognized as an *interaction-acquisition* process in which the individual, himself, plays an important role. In this respect we have seen that the individual's sex, the affective relationships he establishes with his parents, his race and social background, and his need to identify with and defer to higher status peers are all individual characteristics which affect his adaptive activities.

Family

The family has long been considered the setting for the first and, quite possibly, some of the most important socialization experiences. However, its role raises a major question in the study of political socialization: Is the family so far removed from the political system that its influence is irrelevant? Is the influence of intermediary agencies such that they effectively counteract the differential effects of family socialization?

One can assume that primary environmental agencies such as the family have a significant impact upon the political system, yet to establish a precise empirical connection is more difficult.

Family Structure and Political Socialization

If one assumes that politically relevant learning does take place within the family, then variations in family power struc-

---

[1] Erving Goffman, *Encounters* (Indianapolis: Bobbs-Merrill, 1961).

ture, which have a potential impact on patterns of influence, become important points of inquiry.

The power structure in the family can be viewed from at least two perspectives. The first is the authority or decision-making structure which varies to the degree that it includes the children as decision participants. The second is the power relations between parents and the impact that different patterns of conjugal power have on children. Although the politically relevant effect on the offspring of variations in these two types of family structures provides the grist for the first part of the study, the conjugal power relations receives the main force of the analysis.

The Autocratic Family

Scholars have investigated the influence of authoritarian child rearing practices on attitudes and behavior. Recently, social scientists have begun to examine the relations between strict parental control and political deviancy, or what is more popularly called "rebellion" among adolescents. The findings, however, have been mixed. One problem appears to revolve around the question of political saliency. When politics is not important in the family it becomes less an object or target of protest, and rebellion against autocratic parental rule is likely to be manifested in other ways.

Among the political orientations held by the parents, their party identification stands out as the most visible and possibly most salient object of protest. In the Caribbean sample, we were able to measure the strictness and rigidity of parental control, to elicit the party identification of both parents and children, and to determine the level of family or parental politicization.

In the Jamaican culture an increase in family authoritarianism corresponds with an increase in students' deviancy from the party preferences of their parents—until we reach the category that includes the most autocratic parents. Students from these families rival students from the least authoritarian families in their compliance with parental norms. What we may be witnessing is the previously undiscovered effect of a *conformity-rebellion threshold* of family authoritarianism. The same curvilinear pattern and threshold emerges when a control for family politicization is used. Apparently parental dominance in the most autocratic household is so oppressive that it discourages rather than encourages political deviancy.

The few empirical studies on the relations of overstrict parental training methods to political deviancy suggest that deviancy will be greater when the family is politicized, in other words, when politics is available as an object of protest. Our data are only partially consistent with these findings. While, as suggested, differences in culture and methodology may account for some of this variation, the basic relationships seem more complex than originally construed. It is true that among the most authoritarian families offspring deviance increases with family politicization. This is consistent with the general hypothesis. However, the relations between autocratic parents, adolescent party deviation, and family politicization is more complex. Although higher politicization increases student deviancy in the most autocratic families, it has the opposite effect among parents in more permissive households. That is, among the relatively more permissive parents outside the extreme category on the autocratic family measure, parental political interest acts as a catalyst in transmitting and maintaining partisan homogeneity in the family. This is closer to our intuitive notions on how the level of politicization might influence partisan homogeneity. Thus, only in the most oppressively autocratic households does politicization increase deviancy by illuminating party identification as an object of protest.

Parental Power and Maternal Dominance

Maternal dominance appears to have a significant impact on political learning among children. While the magnitude of the differences have not always been great, they have been consistent across national cultures in both mother-only and nuclear families.

In the Caribbean, as in most less industrialized countries, the incidence of mother-only, or maternal, families is quite high. In Jamaica, at least 25 per cent of the families are of this type.

We hypothesized that children reared in these maternal

families might differ politically from children raised in nuclear households in which both mother and father are present. We expected to find that children from maternal families were more authoritarian in their outlook, felt less politically efficacious, and were less interested in politics. In addition, we suspected that male respondents would be more affected than female students by the environment of the maternal family and the absence of the father. After establishing the political relevance of the dependent variables, we tested the hypotheses with controls for social class.

Students from maternal families in the Caribbean proved to be more authoritarian, less politically interested, and less efficacious than those from nuclear families. The pattern is less apparent among the upper classes, but only for efficacy is the maternal effect exclusively a working class phenomenon. Here, the political culture of the more efficacious middle and upper class counteracts the effect of maternal dominance.

A predicted cross-sex pattern develops in which the absence of the father and maternal domination increase authoritarian attitudes and decrease political interest among male students, while this has little effect on females. With political efficacy, however, there is no sex differentiation. Both boys and girls from mother-only families are less efficacious than children from nuclear families.

The relevance of family experiences for the political system depends heavily on the extent to which this political learning is mediated by the intermediary socialization agencies within the society. The stability of these early learned political orientations provides the important link between the family and the larger political system. Tracing the influence of early socialization in maternal and nuclear families as the student moves through the secondary school reveals that children from maternal households enter high school with a higher level of authoritarianism and feel less politically interested and efficacious than those from nuclear families. More important, this relationship continues through the twelfth grade. Thus the maternal effect endures the secondary school experience and remains a significant variable explaining an adolescent's perception of his role in the political process as he is about to enter adulthood.

An analog to the mother-only family is the nuclear family where mother plays a more dominant role than father. We examined data from a national cross section of parents of high school seniors in the United States. There were important similarities between the findings in the United States and those in the Caribbean.

Males from nuclear families in which the mother dominates are not as politically interested and efficacious, and are less likely to engage in political activity than those from father-dominant households. This relationship weakens and tends to reverse itself slightly among the highly educated families.

In the Caribbean as well as the United States maternal dominance is detrimental to male offspring—particularly among the least educated families. Generally conjugal power relations have little political consequence for females.

Mothers Versus Fathers in the Formation of Political Orientations

Next we examined the relative influence of mother and father in *directly* transmitting their political orientations to their offspring.

The prevailing view on intra-familial political involvement in the United States is that the father plays the most active role. Men are more visible politically at the mass and leadership level, and politics is generally assumed to be sex-appropriate for men, whereas doubts prevail regarding women in politics. Therefore, within the family father will probably have more influence over the childrens' political values than mother.

To investigate this hypothesis we used data from that one-third of the national sample of American high school seniors in which *both* parents, as well as the student-offspring, were interviewed. Three major family configurations are produced by combining responses to the party identification questions. First, mother, father, and student all share the same party preference; second, mother and father agree but the student differs; finally, parents are heterogeneous and the child agrees with one or neither.

To illuminate more fully the differential influence of

mothers and fathers we first examined the most ubiquitous parental constellation: the case in which parents share the same party identification. Then we investigated the most appropriate parental combination for the analysis—those families in which mother and father differ in party preference. Here parent-child agreement is scrutinized in a variety of partisan combinations, including the familial properties which accompany different transmission patterns. Because channels of influence found in party attachments may extend to other political orientations as well, we also investigated the relative pull of each parent in selected issue areas.

Our first aim was to find if one parent was more influential than the other in preventing the child from leaving the partisan fold. Contrary to the prevailing view of the political dominance of the father, indices depicting the relative politicization and education of mothers versus fathers revealed that father had only a marginal role in helping preserve triadic homogeneity. If either parent plays the more impressive role, it is the mother. When she is relatively more politicized or educated than the father, triadic homogeneity is maintained more often than when the opposite prevails.

Next we turned to those instances when mother and father had differing party identification. Such parental pairs consisted of conflicting combinations among the three positions of Democrat, Republican, and Independent (pure), which can be summarized into partisan-Independent mixes, and the more extreme bi-polar constellation. The findings in both family types provide additional evidence that fathers are by no means the decisive force in establishing childrens' party identification. American students fail to gravitate in disproportionate numbers to the party of their father. Instead, there is a modest counter-movement which holds regardless of the family combination or the partisan position of the parent.

Certain parental properties accompany these transmission patterns. For example, sex combinations have a bearing on the level of inter-generational agreement. Mother-daughter agreement is highest, while the son's partisan preference is generally split more evenly between the parents. One reason for the mother's strong competitive position appeared to lie in the natural reservoir of affective ties between mother and child. The mother also benefits when she is relatively more politicized, the family is more educated, and she is relatively more intense in her partisanship. Among the five explanatory variables, mother-child closeness proves most stable when controlled for by the other variables.

To see if patterns of maternal transmission extend to areas other than party identification, six issue questions were asked all triad members. Parents who took opposing issue positions were selected out for analysis. Here again the pattern of parent-student issue agreement is contrary to the father-dominant model of value transmission. On each issue the student is more inclined to follow his mother.

Although one should be cautious in generalizing these findings, recall data from an independent sample of the American adult electorate conducted by the Survey Research Center in 1964 support our findings.

The maternal edge reflected in both American samples is found also among Caribbean students. Those respondents who report that their parents support different parties generally agree with their mother more than their father. As in the United States, the mother's advantage increases slightly as parental education increases.

School: Formal Environment

Although schools are considered important instruments of political socialization, there has been very little systematic investigation of the impact of such aspects of the total school milieu as curriculum, teachers, school climate, and peer groups. All may contribute to the political socialization process, but the contribution of each is unclear.

The classroom teacher may be relatively weak as a transmitter of political values to adolescents—a fact which the literature as well as indirect evidence from our data supports. On the other hand, the civics curriculum has been traditionally viewed as an important source of citizenship training.

Past attempts to assess the actual impact of high school curriculum have produced generally inconclusive results. Moreover, the socialization potential of secondary schools is open to question, since the political orientations of many students may be well-formed by the time they reach this level. It is also possible that high school civics courses offer little that is new to the student, but simply provide another layer of redundant information. If one accepts either of these points, dramatic changes in beliefs on the basis of one or two courses should not be expected. However, some movement should be visible.

We investigated this possibility by examining the effect of the civics curriculum on the political orientations of American students. The data came from the national survey of high school seniors. The analysis centered on the relations between the number of civics courses taken and students' political knowledge and sophistication, interest, discussion, media consumption, efficacy and cynicism, as well as their level of civic tolerance and perception of the "good citizen." Multi-variate analysis was used to control seven potentially intervening variables.

The findings were divided into three parts. First, an overview of the results offers little support for the impact of the curriculum even as a minor source of political socialization. Among the entire sample we did not find a single case, out of the ten investigated, in which civics training was significantly associated with students' political orientations.

Second, the absence of positive relationships raises an important question concerning the ubiquitous correlations between years of education and political orientations so common in the literature, particularly the differences between people with high school versus those with college education. High school seniors who are likely to go on to college already differ in politically important ways from their school-mates who will terminate their formal education at the high school level. If we wait until this group enters college to compare its political orientations with those who completed high school only and, of course, charge the difference to the effects of higher education, we are seriously confusing the effects of selection and political socialization.

Third, although our overall findings are unambiguous, it seems that, under special conditions, civics courses do have an impact on American high school students. When White and Negro students are observed separately, the curriculum clearly exerts more influence on the latter.

One significant explanation of the singular consequences of the curriculum for Negro students is that information redundancy is lower for them than for Whites. Because of cultural and social status differences, Negroes are more likely to encounter new or conflicting perspectives, whereas White students generally receive already familiar materials.

School and Peer Group: Informal Environment

The general lack of positive evidence concerning the curriculum led us into a relatively untilled area: the informal milieu of the peer group and school. We questioned whether homogeneous class peer groups and schools reinforce the class way of life and associated political orientations of their members, while heterogeneous or mixed class environments provide students with an opportunity to learn from peers who have different styles and outlooks.

We hypothesized that a major socializing function of homogeneous class peer groups and schools was to reinforce the political culture of the lower classes, and thus, to maintain existing political and cultural cleavages. In heterogeneous peer groups and schools, on the other hand, higher class students are in a position to bestow approval on those of lower status. Therefore, opinions among these working class students are likely to be re-socialized in the direction of those held by higher-status peers.

In Jamaica class cleavages are reinforced and exaggerated among working class students in homogeneous peer groups. On every political variable, these students assume an attitudinal position farther from that of the middle and upper classes than the positions of the working class in general. By comparison, heterogeneous class peer groups consistently re-socialize the working class toward the level of politicization and general political outlook of the higher social classes.

The school, as well as the peer group, may maintain class

differences because it is composed of students of the same social class. But if students from various class backgrounds are assigned to a school, the resulting milieu may promote the political re-socialization of the working class. To test this hypothesis, schools in the Caribbean sample were ordered by their class environment in a way analogous to the ordering of the peer groups.

Again, a familiar pattern develops. Homogeneous class schools reinforce the norms of the lower classes, while maintaining the political cleavage between them and the middle and upper classes. With the exception of economic attitudes, heterogeneous schools re-socialize working class students in the direction of higher class political values.

We found that middle class students react to mixed peer groups in the same way as lower class students do. They defer in the direction of the upper class members. The relationships are consistently weaker, however, particularly on the economic issues. Upper class students, however, who have even less reason to defer and fewer higher-status peer-mates with whom to interact, are not affected significantly by class mixing. In addition, school-class climate has no impact on the political values of either the middle or upper class. Only among the working class are *both* peer group and school important.

To judge if school-class climate outside the peer group contributed to the peer group's reported effect, and to see if class mixing in both agencies is cumulative, we re-examined the relationships under controlled conditions.

Clearly, in each agency a heterogeneous class environment has an independent as well as a cumulative effect on the political orientations of working class students in the Caribbean. The direction of change is consistently toward the political culture of the higher classes. Equally important, a straight comparison between the political culture of the undifferentiated working class and the higher classes obviously tends to underestimate the cleavages in a society, since the political cleavage between students in both homogeneous peer groups and schools and the higher classes is much greater.

Although there has been little empirical study of the

political effect of class mixing in the United States, we were fortunate in securing data from a sample of students in Detroit, Michigan which allowed us to expand on the potential influence of the class milieu in American schools. The schools in the Detroit study were ordered by their class environment, as were the schools in the Caribbean sample. The relationship we found is part of a consistent pattern: the re-socialization of working class students in mixed schools in the direction of higher class political norms.

Influence of Different Agencies

Most political socialization research has confined itself to single agency analysis. To speak of the *relative* influence of agencies, however, assumes that we are able to sum their individual effects and then compare summations. This in turn assumes more progress than we have made to date, since we are still in the process of isolating different characteristics of these institutions and their relationships to politics. At this stage when one refers to relative influence, it usually means a comparison of the socialization effects of selected aspects of one agency with similar characteristics, or at least causally linked characteristics, in others.

Although the question of relative or differential influence remains essentially untouched, the problem is at least recognized in the literature. This is more than can be said for another provocative question which concerns the possibility that the influence of an agency may be concentrated within a particular *level* of the politically relevant dimension under study, and that exposure to a number of agencies may be necessary to move people along the total length of this dimension. For example, the model pattern in the United States may be that a certain constellation of family characteristics is important in moving offspring from a low to a medium level of political interest. But at this point the family has reached the zenith of its influence, and now other secondary agencies with certain identifiable characteristics are required to move children to a higher level of interest.

In the last chapter we used a form of conditional probability analysis to probe both questions within a single model, using the Caribbean sample.

First, we established the political relevance of our dependent variable, political efficacy. Then we proceeded (1) to estimate the relative role of a politicized environment in family, school, and peer group upon the development of political efficacy, and (2) to determine how these different agencies affect each level of the dependent variable.

The family accounts for almost four times more movement along the entire efficacy scale than either the peer group or school, and as we saw, is the *only* agency which moves students along the whole range of the efficacy scale: from low to medium to high. Although its relative influence declined among the upper classes, it still maintains its dominance in the low-to-medium range. Only in the medium-to-high range among the upper class does the family succumb to the greater influence of the peer group.

Although the family moves students along the entire efficacy dimension, the school and peer group operate at different ends of this scale. The wider school environment, for example, functions almost exclusively in the low-to-medium range, while the face-to-face peer group concentrates on what may be the most difficult and politically relevant socialization task: moving students from a medium to a high sense of political efficacy.

Although our findings may not be exactly duplicated in other cultures, it seems possible that the truncated role of the different agents is descriptive of a general phenomenon which characterizes the entire socialization process. At a minimum, building such considerations such as these into our models may prove useful in exposing the relative, possibly truncated, role of various agencies in the political socialization process.

Political Socialization and the
Implementation of Values in the Political System

While we accept as normal the constant revision of the school curriculum by unknown educators, many of us rebel at the suggestion that we formally begin to manipulate the social environment to inculcate *particular* values or implement certain goals. Somehow the "natural," or more accurately the random, socialization process has taken on a moral quality of its own. Many think directed social change smacks of *1984*. However this stance overlooks the fact that considerable social manipulation, for better or for worse, is taking place any way. The definition of the model American, for example, has been accepted as the legitimate concern of government and community since the inception of the Republic. Our churches have been accorded considerable authority in the specification of ethical behavior.

Social scientists often go to great lengths to avoid the implications of their research for the implementation of values. In an area such as political socialization, where potential points of intervention are constantly being discovered, this stance seems particularly risky. The possibility for the application of research findings is immediate and certainly should be preceded by a discussion of the *values* to be inculcated and the *proper means* to this end.

Here, it is interesting to note that what are often considered to be legitimate points of leverage in the study and encouragement of political and economic development in other countries—presumably worthwhile goals—are often taboo in our own. While this may make the Western man's burden easier to bear at home it bespeaks of a certain international callousness.

This is not to deny our interest in the determinants of political development. We seek deeper insight into the socialization-polity relationship, in both historical and comparative perspectives, not only because of our theoretical interest in patterns of political change, but also because we have an immediate practical interest in the direction of political evolution. Therefore it seems useful to illustrate how some of our findings bear on certain practical problems of political development.

Administrators or citizens interested in the evolution of their polity first must ask themselves which values and behavior they wish to inculcate or maintain: political attitudes supportive of the government or regime, tolerance of the civil rights of others, reverence for hard work and thrift, a sense of political efficacy, and so forth. The answers will depend to some degree on the linkages established between the specific phenomena and the larger system goals. The linkages themselves may be the products of other research not specifically connected to the study of political socialization.

Once the desired values and behavior patterns have been specified, and we are fully aware of the difficulty here, we begin our search for the environmental factors predictive of these patterns. Direct linkages may be established with selected characteristics of the socialization agents, or psychological dispositions may intervene, which add to the predictive power. For example, assume that we desire to decrease ambivalent feelings toward the regime, and find that ambivalence is related to certain environmental conditions in a socialization agent through feelings of personal ineffectiveness.

A model such as the one in Chapter 6 seems particularly useful in searching for those agents in which one could most profitably exert the leverage necessary to the inculcation of desired attitudes. The model assessed the relative impact of a number of agents on the development of political efficacy among high school students in the Caribbean, who, like those in other less industrialized countries, are an elite group. The total socialization environment was sufficiently strong to move a majority of these students into the medium efficacy range. An important part of this process involved the politicized environment of the family and school, which together accounted for the placement of 43 per cent of all students at the medium efficacy level. The socialization process as a whole proved less effective in the upper efficacy range. As in most countries, it was able to provide only a small corps of adolescents with a high sense of efficacy. In this context, our findings take on added significance, since the family and peer group alone account for the placement of 82 per cent of all students found at the higher level. Clearly, the incidence of family and peer group politicization has an important bearing on the national distribution of high political efficacy among an important strata of the population in this developing country.

In the specification of relevant socialization agencies for the policy-maker, it is apparent that while the manipulation of institutions may be desirable and theoretically possible, the realistic alternatives available to the government official make the control of some agents more politically feasible than others. Clearly, the school system which normally has administrative connections with the state is more tractable than the family. Among many students of development, formal education is

> the prime determinant of the total developmental process, as the master instrument for changing attitudes, for transforming social structures, for sparking or accelerating economic growth, and for determining new political patterns.[2]

There is also considerable discussion in the development literature about whether curriculum should be exclusively scientific and technical or humanistic and legal, as well as what is the best "mix" to assure political stability. Our findings in American high schools are not optimistic about curriculum as a major source of political socialization. Unless there is a radical restructuring of civics courses to reduce information redundancy, one must expect them to contribute little to the socialization process.

In societies at different stages of development from the United States, however, traditional norms often clash with the modern values promoted by the political elites. Under these conditions where information redundancy is low, policy makers may lean heavily on the formal curriculum as an agent of change. But, as with upper class Negroes in the United States, there can be unanticipated consequences which policy makers may wish to avoid. This means that social experimentation must precede more massive attempts at direction.

While the findings on the effect of the formal school environment are inconclusive, the informal class milieu of peer groups and schools appears to be an important agent of

[2] James S. Coleman, *Education and Political Development*, p. 522.

change. The problem is how to take advantage of the power of these agencies to induce change in ways that move in the direction of our general developmental goals.

Certainly homogeneous class schools and peer groups help maintain class cleavages in a polity with the potential for conflict, while a heterogeneous class environment provides a vehicle for introducing "modernizing" norms to large social groups. But the exact nature and success of this process depends largely on the direction in which deference moves and on the political beliefs of those with higher status. Although deference usually flows from lower to higher classes, there is no reason to believe that in societies with more prolitarian norms it would not move in the opposite direction or at least more horizontally. Any intention to manipulate peer grouping or class environment within the school should obviously be based on a careful calculus of one's objectives and the political values of the different classes.

If, for example, social planners in the Caribbean felt that the task of industrialization required two immediate political goals, namely (1) to maintain a climate of political support for the regime and (2) to discourage—by non-coercive means—excessive political participation, they would do well to segregate working class students from those of higher classes, because, as public education is expanded, and working class students are allowed to mingle with their higher-status peers, they become more politicized and less supportive of the political regime. This could become a potentially critical output in developing political systems. On the other hand, by maintaining separate facilities, the polity forsakes some of its leverage in creating greater support for civil liberties and democratic values among the working class. However, as seen earlier, the purity of the latter's more liberal economic views is compromised by associating with highter-status peers.

Clearly, neither solution will satisfy all parties. Although segregation is more machiavellian, it is undoubtedly closer to the twin goals of political stability and industrialization implicit in the writings of most students of development.

The family is much less approachable than schools and student peer groups. Even in totalitarian societies it has remained one of the major obstacles to total control. This does not mean that non-coercive means cannot be used to penetrate its shell. For example, a constant theme in this book was the politically relevant role played by mothers. Mother-only families make up a significant percentage of the households in less industrialized countries. If maternal dominance represents an important social cost and is contrary to developmental goals because it lowers political efficacy and interest, it is incumbent upon the political elite to provide employment for adult males so that they will not be denied the dual but culturally linked role of father, husband, and provider.

Both in the United States and the Caribbean, the mother equaled or surpassed the father in the direct transfer of political orientations to the children. We have, it seems overlooked mother's control of resources in the family and her natural affective ties with the children, both of which buttress her position as an important inculcator of political norms. Special appeals to women by way of the media, Parent Teacher Organization, child care, and home economic institutes, and so forth, all provide points of contact for the government.

In conclusion, although the question of social control cannot escape its Orwellian connotations, the wise citizen and responsible public servant can enjoy unprecedented prerogatives for useful and humane intervention in the evolution of political systems. My foregoing remarks on the relevance of political socialization for the implementation of values may provide a sense of the possibilities, and hopefully this research has extended the base of our accumulated knowledge, at the same time mapping somewhat more thoroughly the contribution of selected primary and secondary agencies to the political socialization process.

Data regarding the socialization process in the Caribbean were collected through interviews and questionnaires administered to a multi-stage national sample of 1287 Jamaican secondary school students during Spring 1964.

The multi-stage sample design was based on a stratified cluster sample of unequal clusters.[1] To ensure an adequate representation of class backgrounds and family structures, a panel of educators was asked to stratify the population of 41 government aided schools as to the estimated class background of the students in attendance. Schools were classified into high, intermediate, and low status on the basis of the panel's recommendations. It was later found that there was a high correlation between the status of the school as ranked by informants and the socio-economic status of the students as measured by objective indicators taken from the individual data.

Among this population of government schools 14 were female, 7 male, and 20 coeducational. In the mixed or coeducational schools 56 per cent of the students were female and 44 per cent male.[2] Since it was not desirable to have an unduly heavy loading of females in the sample it was decided to eliminate girls' schools from the sample population. This left 27 schools with a total population of 13,483 males and females.

[1] Frederick F. Stephan and Philip J. McCarthy, *Sampling Opinions: An Analysis of Survey Procedures* (New York: Wiley, 1958), pp. 200–07.

[2] Data supplied by private communication from the Ministry of Education, Government of Jamaica, Kingston, 1964.

A sample of schools was randomly drawn from each strata of the population of mixed and male schools. These schools were distributed throughout the Kingston metropolitan area, the rural areas, and one was located in a middle-sized Jamaican city. Next, all students in the first, fourth, and fifth forms were administered questionnaires. Since the Jamaican secondary school is patterned after the British grammar school rather than the American high school, these forms are comparable to grades eight, eleven, and twelve in the American school system.

This type of sampling procedure allows each student in the population a known probability of being selected. The level of generality of the analytical results is intended to be broad enough to apply to students in government secondary schools throughout Jamaica, with the exception of those who attend all-girls' schools. However, because such a large percentage of females was included in the sample of mixed schools, the findings from our sample can be generalized, with some confidence, to all females in government secondary schools.

The fact that eighth as well as eleventh- and twelfth-grade student cross-sections were collected facilitates the inferences we can make concerning the stability of attitudes and behavior over time.

Such quasi-longitudinal assumptions, however, obviously necessitate data on the rate and background of dropouts. Although the Jamaican Ministry of Education had no reliable statistics on dropouts, the headmasters of each of the schools were able to provide the necessary information. There was some student movement between government aided schools as families moved, but in no school was the net dropout rate more than 3 per cent from the eighth to the twelfth grade. Obviously, Jamaican students do not take lightly that they are among the select 6 per cent (N = 16,300) of the total population of secondary school age who have been given the opportunity to attend government aided secondary schools.[3]

[3] To the 6 per cent should be added another 4 per cent who attend private secondary schools. With a few notable exceptions, the hodge-podge of private secondary schools are inferior to government schools in

Headmasters were unable to give precise information on the background of the dropouts, but estimated that most students dropped out because they were unable to do the academic work, the rest left school for monetary reasons. In either case, the percentages are so slight that dropouts have no significant effect on the quasi-longitudinal assumptions made in this analysis.

---

quality of education, qualifications of teachers, and generally enjoy a much lower status in the eyes of the Jamaicans. O. C. Francis, *The People of Modern Jamaica* (Kingston, Jamaica: Department of Statistics, 1963), Tables 1.7 and 3.9.

These percentages are based on the 1960 Jamaican national census. In private communications, the Jamaican Ministry of Education estimated that as of January, 1964, the number of students in government secondary schools was approximately 21,000. No comparable figures are available on the increase in the population of secondary school age. However, it is unlikely that the percentage of the population attending government aided schools has changed appreciably. Some political commentators in Jamaica have even suggested that it has declined.

Student-Parent Identification Agreement*

	(1)	(2)	(3)	(4)	(5)	(6)	(7)	(8)	(9)	Total Row Per Cent	N
MOTHER	Democrat	Democrat	Independent	Republican	Independent	Democrat	Independent	Republican	Republican		
FATHER	Democrat	Independent	Democrat	Democrat	Independent	Republican	Republican	Independent	Republican		
Strong Democrat	29.6	7.0	0.0	3.4	0.0	8.2	0.0	0.0	1.5	14.9	75
Weak Democrat	35.9	24.0	24.4	10.3	8.5	13.6	36.4	0.0	7.4	23.0	116
Independent Democrat	19.3	20.0	14.4	15.0	33.1	22.6	6.6	21.4	9.8	16.7	83
SUBTOTAL	(84.8)	(51.0)	(38.8)	(28.7)	(41.6)	(44.4)	(43.0)	(21.4)	(18.7)	(54.6)	(274)
Independent subtotal	(8.2)	(37.0)	(39.8)	(38.6)	(8.5)	(20.7)	(17.2)	(33.6)	(13.4)	(15.3)	(76)
Independent Republican	1.0	12.0	0.0	4.3	28.8	17.4	23.8	37.9	21.1	10.4	52
Weak Republican	2.9	0.0	16.4	22.7	21.2	17.4	9.3	7.1	22.4	11.2	56
Strong Republican	3.2	0.0	5.0	5.6	0.0	0.0	6.6	0.0	24.4	8.5	42
SUBTOTAL	(7.1)	(12.0)	(21.4)	(32.6)	(50.0)	(34.8)	(39.7)	(45.0)	(67.9)	(30.1)	(150)
TOTAL PER CENT	100.1	100.0	100.0	99.9	100.1	99.9	99.9	100.0	100.0	100.0	
Number cases	228	20	20	23	12	37	15	14	131		500
Proportion of sample	45.6	4.0	4.0	4.7	2.4	7.3	3.0	2.8	26.2		

Student's Party Identification (left-axis label)

*A Democratic or Republican parent includes those who are strong, weak, and Independent leaners. Independents include only pure Independents. Tau-b = .51.

Key:

(a) homogeneous parents, child agrees
(b) homogeneous parents, deviating child
(c) partisan-Independent parents
(d) bi-polar parents

Aberle, David F. "Culture and Socialization," in Francis L. K. Hsu (ed.), *Psychological Anthropology*. Homewood, Illinois: Dorsey Press, 1961, pp. 381–99.

Abrams, Philip and Alan Little. "The Young Voter in British Politics," *British Journal of Sociology*, 16 (1965), 95–110.

Adelson, Joseph and Robert O'Neil. "The Growth of Political Ideas in Adolescence: The Sense of Community," *Journal of Personality and Social Psychology*, 4 (September, 1966), 295–306.

Agger, Robert E., Marshall Goldstein, and Stanley Pearl. "Political Cynicism: Measurement and Meaning," *Journal of Politics*, 23 (August, 1961), 477–506.

Almond, Gabriel and James S. Coleman. *The Politics of the Developing Areas*. Princeton: Princeton University Press, 1960.

——— and Sidney Verba. *The Civic Culture*. Princeton: Princeton University Press, 1963.

Andrews, Frank, James Morgan, and John Sonquist. *Multiple Classification Analysis*. Ann Arbor: Institute for Social Research, University of Michigan, 1967.

Argyle, M. and P. Delin. "Non-universal Laws of Socialization," *Human Relations*, 18 (February, 1965), 77–86.

Azrael, Jeremy R. "Patterns of Polity Directed Educational Development: The Soviet Union," in James S. Coleman (ed.), *Education and Political Development*. Princeton: Princeton University Press, 1965, pp. 233–71.

Bach, George R. "Father-Fantasies and Father-Typing in Father Separated Children," *Child Development*, 17 (March-June, 1946), 63–79.

Baldwin, Alfred L. "Socialization and Parent-Child Relationship," *Child Development*, 19 (September, 1948), 127–36.

Bales, Robert F. *Family Socialization and the Interaction Process*. Glencoe: Free Press, 1955.

Banfield, D. C. *The Moral Basis of a Backward Society*. Glencoe: Free Press, 1958.

Barber, James David. *The Lawmakers: Recruitment and Adaptation to Legislative Life*. New Haven: Yale University Press, 1965.

Barton, Allen H. *Studying the Effects of College Education*. New Haven: Edward Hazen Foundation, 1959.

Baur, E. Jackson. "Public Opinion and the Primary Group," *American Sociological Review*, 25 (April, 1960), 208–19.

Becker, H. S. "Social-Class Variations in the Teacher-Pupil Relationship," *Journal of Educational Sociology*, 25 (April, 1952), 451–65.

Bender, Gerald. "Political Socialization and Political Change," *Western Political Quarterly*, 20 (June, 1967), 390–407.

Bereday, George Z. "Education and Youth," *The Satellites in Eastern Europe*, H. L. Roberts (ed.), in *The Annals of the American Academy of Political and Social Science*, 317 (1958), 63–70.

———. "Introduction" and "Notes," in Charles Merriam, *The Making of Citizens: Comparative Education Studies*. New York: Teachers College Press, 1966.

——— and Bonnie B. Stretch. "Political Education in the U.S.A. and USSR," *Comparative Education Review*, 7 (1963), 9–16.

Berelson, Bernard, *et al. Voting*. Chicago: University of Chicago Press, 1954.

Binder, Leonard. "Egypt: The Integrative Revolution," in Lucian Pye and Sidney Verba (eds.), *Political Culture and Political Development*. Princeton: Princeton University Press, 1965, pp. 407–19.

Blalock, Herbert, Jr. *Causal Inferences in Non-Experimental Research*. Chapel Hill: University of North Carolina Press, 1964.

Blood, Robert and Donald Wolfe. *Husbands and Wives*. Glencoe; Free Press, 1960.

Bloom, Benjamin S. *Stability and Change in Human Characteristics*. New York: Wiley, 1965.

Bonilla, Frank. "Student Politics in Latin America," *PROD*, 3 (1959–1960), 12–15.

Borgatta, Edgar. "Role-Playing Specification, Personality, and Performance," *Sociometry*, 24 (1961), 218–33.

Bowerman, Charles E. and John W. Kinch. "Changes in Family and Peer Orientations of Children Between the Fourth and Tenth Grades," *Social Forces*, 37 (March, 1959), 206–11.

Brim, Orville G. Jr. "Socialization Through the Life Cycle," *Items*, 18 (March, 1964), 1–5.

————. "Personality Development as Role Learning," in I. Iscoe and H. Stevenson (eds.), *Personality Development in Children*. Austin: University of Texas Press, 1960, pp. 127–59.

———— and Stanton Wheeler. *Socialization After Childhood: Two Essays*. New York: Wiley, 1966.

Brink, William and Louis Harris. *The Negro Revolution in America*. New York: Simon & Schuster, 1964.

Bronfenbrenner, Urie. "Freudian Theories of Identification and Their Derivatives," *Child Development*, 31 (1958), 15–40.

————. "Socialization and Social Class Through Time and Space," in E. E. Maccoby, *et al.*, *Readings in Social Psychology*. New York: Holt, 1958, pp. 400–24.

————. "Some Familial Antecedents of Responsibility and Leadership in Adolescents," in Luigi Petrullo and Bernard Bass (eds.), *Leadership and Interpersonal Behavior*. New York: Holt, 1961, pp. 237–89.

Brown, Claude. *Man Child in the Promised Land*. New York: Macmillan, 1965.

Brown, J. C. "Education of the French Administrative Class," *Public Personnel Review*, 16 (January, 1955), 17–27.

Browning, Rufus and Herbert Jacob. "Power Motivations and the Political Personality," *Public Opinion Quarterly*, 28 (Spring, 1964), 75–90.

Brzezinski, Zbigniew and Samuel P. Huntington. *Political Power: U.S.A./U.S.S.R.* New York: Viking, 1963.

Burton, Roger and John Whiting. "The Absent Father and Cross-Sex Identity," *Merrill-Palmer Quarterly*, 7 (April, 1961), 84–95.

Byrne, Donn. "Parental Antecedents of Authoritarianism," *Journal of Personality and Social Psychology*, 1 (1965), 369–73.

Campbell, Angus, *et al. Elections and the Political Order*. New York: Wiley, 1966.

————. *The American Voter*. New York: Wiley, 1960.

————. *The Voter Decides*. Evanston, Illinois: Row, Peterson, 1954.

————, Gerald Gurin, and Warren Miller. "Political Efficacy and Political Participation," in Heinz Eulau, Samuel Eldersveld, and Morris Janowitz (eds.), *Political Behavior*. Glencoe: Free Press, 1959, pp. 170–74.

Campbell, J. "Peer Relations in Childhood," in M. Hoffman and L. Hoffman (eds.), *Review of Child Research Literature*, 1, New York: Russell Sage Foundation, 1964.

Central Office of Information. *Jamaica: The Making of a Nation*. London: Her Majesty's Stationery Office, 1962.

Chapanis, N. and Chapanis, A. "Cognitive Dissonance: Five Years Later," *Psychological Bulletin*, 61 (1964), 1–22.

Chapman, Ames W. "Attitudes Toward Legal Authorities by Juveniles," *Sociology and Social Research*, 40 (1956), 170–75.

Child, Irvin L. "Socialization," in Gardner Lindzey (ed.), *Handbook of Social Psychology*. Cambridge: Addison-Wesley, 1954, pp. 655–92.

Clark, Kenneth B. *Dark Ghetto*. New York: Harper, 1965.

Clark, Nadine I., *et al. Civics for Americans*. New York: Macmillan, 1965.

Clark, Edith. *My Mother Who Fathered Me*. London: Allen and Unwin, 1957.

Clausen, John A. "Research on Socialization and Personality Development in the United States and France: Remarks on the Paper by Professor Chombart de Lauwe," *American Sociological Review*, 31 (1966), 248–57.

Coleman, James S. "Education and the Political Scientist," *Items*, 19 (1965), 5–7.

————. "Introduction," in James S. Coleman (ed.), *Education and Political Development*. Princeton: Princeton University Press, 1965, pp. 18–25.

————. *Introduction to Mathematical Sociology*. Glencoe: Free Press, 1964.

————. *The Adolescent Society*. New York: Free Press, 1961.

Collier, R. M. and H. P. Lawrence. "The Adolescent Feeling of Psychological Isolation," *Educational Theory*, 2 (August, 1951), 110.

Converse, Philip E. "The Nature of Belief Systems in Mass

Publics," in David Apter (ed.), *Ideology and Discontent*. New York: Free Press, 1964, pp. 206–61.

———. "The Shifting Role of Class" in E. Hartley, *Readings in Social Psychology*, 3rd ed., New York: Holt, 1958, pp. 388–99.

——— and Georges Dupuex. "Politicization of the Electorate in France and the United States," *Public Opinion Quarterly*, 26 (1962), 23.

Cox, C. Benjamin and Jack E. Cousins. "Teaching Social Studies in Secondary Schools and Colleges," in Byron Massialas and Frederick R. Smith (eds.), *New Challenges in the Social Studies*. Belmont, California: Wadsworth, 1965, Chapter 4.

Crespi, Leo P. "German Youth and Adults View Individual Responsibility," *International Journal of Opinion and Attitude Research*, 2 (1948), 230–36.

Crittenden, John. "Aging and Party Affiliation," *Public Opinion Quarterly*, 26 (1962), 648–57.

———. "Aging and Political Participation," *Western Political Quarterly*, 16 (1962), 323–31.

Cuffaro, Harriet K. "Reaction of Preschool Children to the Assassination of President Kennedy," *Young Children*, 20 (1964–1965), 100–5.

Davies, A. F. "The Child's Discovery of Social Class," *Australia and New Zealand Journal of Sociology*, 1 (1965), 21–27.

Davies, James C. *Human Nature in Politics*. New York: Wiley, 1963.

———. "The Family's Role in Political Socialization," *The Annals*, 361 (September, 1965), 10–19.

Davis, Allison and John Dollard. *Children of Bondage: The Personality Development of Negro Youth in the Urban South*. New York: Harper, 1940.

Dawson, Richard. "Political Socialization," in James A. Robinson (ed.), *Political Science Annual: An International Review*, 1. New York: Bobbs-Merrill, 1966, pp. 1–84.

——— and Kenneth Prewitt. *Aspects of Political Socialization*. Boston: Little, Brown, 1969.

Dennis, Jack. "Major Problems of Political Socialization Research," *Midwest Journal of Political Science*, 12 (February, 1968), 85–114.

Deutsch, M., A. Jensen, and I. Katz (eds.), *Race, Class and Personality Development*. New York: Holt, 1967.

Dickens, Sara Lee and Charles Hobart. "Parental Dominance and Offspring Ethnocentrism," *Journal of Social Psychology*, 49 (May, 1959), 297–303.

Dimond, Stanley E. "Citizenship Education," *Encyclopedia of Educational Research*, 3rd ed. (1960), 206–10.

———— and Elmer F. Pflieger. *Civics for Citizens*. Philadelphia: Lippincott, 1965.

Dodge, Richard W. and Eugene S. Uyeki. "Political Affiliation and Imagery Across Two Related Generations," *Midwest Journal of Political Science*, 6 (1962), 266–76.

Doob, Leonard W. "South Tyrol: An Introduction to the Psychological Syndrome of Nationalism," *Public Opinion Quarterly*, 26 (1962), 172–84.

————. *Patriotism and Nationalism: Their Psychological Foundations*. New Haven: Yale University Press, 1964.

Dore, R. P. "Education: Japan," in Robert E. Ward and Dankwart A. Rustow (eds.), *Political Modernization in Japan and Turkey*. Princeton: Princeton University Press, 1964, pp. 176–204.

Dornbusch, S. M. "The Military Academy as an Assimilating Institution," *Social Forces*, 33 (May, 1955), 316–21.

Douvan, Elizabeth and Martin Gold. "American Adolescence: Model Patterns of Bio-Social Change," in M. Hoffman and L. Hoffman (eds.), *Review of Child Development Research*, 2. New York: Russell Sage Foundation, 1966, pp. 469–528.

Dreger, Ralph M. and Kent S. Miller. "Comparative Psychological Studies of Negro and Whites in the United States," *Psychological Bulletin*, 57, 5 (September, 1960), 361–402.

Drucker, A. J. and H. H. Remmers. "Citizenship Attitudes of Graduated Seniors at Purdue University," *Journal of Educational Psychology*, 42 (1951), 231–35.

Dunn, Stephen and Ethel Dunn. "Directed Cultural Change in the Soviet Union: Some Soviet Studies," *American Anthropologist*, 64 (April, 1962), 328–39.

Easton, David. "An Approach to the Analysis of Political Systems," *World Politics*, 9 (1957), 383–400.

————. *A Systems Analysis of Political Life*. New York: Wiley, 1965.

————. "Function of Formal Education in a Political System," *School Review*, 65 (1957), 3–4, 316.

———— and Jack Dennis. "The Child's Acquisition of Regime

Norms: Political Efficacy," *American Political Science Review*, 61 (March, 1967), 25–38.

——— and Jack Dennis. "The Child's Image of Government," *The Annals of the American Academy of Political and Social Science*, 361 (1965), 40–57.

——— and Robert Hess. "The Child's Political World," *Midwest Journal of Political Science*, 6 (August, 1962), 229–46.

——— and Robert Hess. "Youth and the Political System," in S. Lipset and L. Lowenstein (eds.), *Cultural and Social Character*. New York: Free Press, 1961, pp. 226–51.

Edelstein, Alex S. "Since Bennington: Evidence of Change in Student Political Behavior," *Public Opinion Quarterly*, 26 (1962), 564–77.

Edgar, Earl E. "Kansas Study of Education for Citizenship," *Phi Delta Kappan*, 33 (December, 1951), 175–78.

Educational Politics Commission. *Learning the Ways of Democracy: A Case Book in Civic Education*. Washington: National Education Association of the United States, 1940.

Eisenstadt, Samuel N. *From Generation to Generation*. Glencoe: Free Press, 1956.

Elder, Glen H., Jr. *Adolescent Achievement and Mobility Aspirations*. Chapel Hill: Institute for Research in Social Science, 1962.

———. "Family Structure and Educational Attainment: A Cross-National Analysis," *American Sociological Review*, 30 (February, 1965), 81–96.

———. "Parental Power Legitimation and Its Effects on the Adolescent," *Sociometry*, 26 (March, 1963), 50–65.

———. "Role Relations, Sociocultural Environments and Autocratic Family Ideology," *Sociometry*, 28 (1965), 173–96.

Elder, Joseph W. "National Loyalties in a Newly Independent Nation," in David Apter (ed.), *Ideology and Discontent*. New York: Free Press, 1964, pp. 77–92.

Elkin, Frederick. *The Child and Society*. New York: Random House, 1960.

Erikson, Erik. *Childhood and Society*. New York: Norton, 1950.
———. *Young Man Luther: A Study in Psychoanalysis and History*. New York: Norton, 1958.

Eulau, Heinz, William Buchanan, LeRoy Ferguson, and John C. Wahlke. "The Political Socialization of American State Legislators," *Midwest Journal of Political Science,* 3 (1959), 188–206.

——— and John D. Sprague. *Lawyers in Politics.* New York: Random House, 1963.

Fagen, Richard R. *Cuba: The Political Content of Adult Education.* Stanford: Hoover Institution Studies, 1964.

Fenno, R. "The House Apropriations Committee as a Political System," *American Political Science Review,* 56 (June, 1962), 310–24.

Festinger, Leon. *A Theory of Cognitive Dissonance.* New York: Harper, 1957.

Finney, D. *Probit Analysis.* Cambridge: Cambridge University Press, 1952.

Fischer-Galati, Stephan A. "Communist Indoctrination in Rumanian Elementary Schools," *Harvard Educational Review,* 22 (1952), 191–202.

Francis, O. C. *The People of Modern Jamaica.* Kingston: Jamaican Department of Statistics, 1963.

Freud, Sigmund. *An Outline of Psychoanalysis.* London: Hogarth Press, 1949.

Frey, Frederick W. "Education: Turkey," in Robert E. Ward and Dankwart A. Rustow (eds.), *Political Modernization in Japan and Turkey.* Princeton: Princeton University Press, 1964, pp. 205–35.

Froman, Lewis A. Jr. "Personality and Political Socialization," *Journal of Politics.* 23 (May, 1961), 341–52.

——— and James K. Skipper, Jr. "An Approach to the Learning of Party Identification," *Public Opinion Quarterly,* 27 (1963), 473–80.

Gage, Robert W. "Patriotism and Military Discipline as a Function of Degree of Military Training," *Journal of Social Psychology,* 64 (1964) 101–11.

Geiger, Kent. "Changing Political Attitudes in a Totalitarian Society: A Case Study of the Role of the Family," *World Politics,* 8 (1956), 187–205.

Gill, Lois J. and Bernard Spilka. "Some Non-intellectual Correlates of Academic Achievement Among Mexican-American Secondary School Students," *Journal of Educational Psychology,* 53 (June, 1962), 144–49.

Glenn, Norval D. and J. L. Simmons. "Are Regional Cultural

Values Diminishing?" *Public Opinion Quarterly*, 31 (Summer, 1967), 176–93.

Goffman, Erving. *Encounters: Two Studies in the Sociology of Interaction*. Indianapolis: Bobbs-Merrill, 1961.

Goldrich, Daniel. "Peasants' Sons in City Schools: An Inquiry into the Politics of Urbanization in Panama and Costa Rica," *Human Organization*, 23 (1964), 328–33.

———. "Requisites for Political Legitimacy in Panama," *Public Opinion Quarterly*, 26 (1962), 664–68.

———. *Sons of the Establishment*. New York: Rand McNally, 1966.

——— and Edward W. Scott. "Developing Political Orientations of Panamanian Students," *Journal of Politics*, 23 (1961), 84–107.

Goldsen, Rose, *et al. What College Students Think*. Princeton: Van Nostrand, 1960.

Gordon, C. Wayne. *The Social System of the High School*. Glencoe: Free Press, 1957.

Gorer, Geoffrey. *The American People*. New York: Norton, 1948.

———. *The People of Great Russia*. London: Cresset Press, 1949.

Greenstein, Fred. *Children and Politics*. New Haven: Yale University Press, 1965.

———. "New Light on Changing American Values: A Forgotten Body of Survey Data," *Social Forces*, 42 (1964), 441–50.

———. "Personality and Political Socialization: The Theories of Authoritarian and Democratic Character," *The Annals*, 361 (1965), 81–95.

———. "Political Socialization," *International Encyclopedia of the Social Sciences*. New York: Crowell Collier, 1968.

———. "Popular Images of the President," *American Journal of Psychiatry*, 122 (1965), 523–29.

———. "The Benevolent Leader: Children's Images of Political Authority," *American Political Science Review*, 54 (December, 1960), 934–44.

———. "The Impact of Personality on Politics: An Attempt to Clear Away Underbrush," *American Political Science Review*, 61 (September, 1967), 629–41.

———. "The Psychological Function of the American President for Citizens," in Elmer E. Cornwell, Jr. (ed.), *The American*

Presidency: Vital Center. Chicago: Scott-Foresman, 1966, pp. 30–36.

Grier, William H. and Price M. Cobbs. *Black Rage.* New York: Basic Books, 1968.

Gronseth, E. "The Impact of Father Absence in Sailor Families upon the Personality Structure and Social Adjustment of Adult Sailor Sons," in N. Anderson (ed.), *Studies of the Family,* 2, Part I. Gottingen: Vanderhoeck and Ruprecht, 1957, pp. 97–114.

Grossholtz, Jean. *Politics in the Philippines.* Boston: Little, Brown, 1964.

Harvey, J. and J. M. Rutherford. "Status in the Informal Group: Influence and Influencibility at Different Age Levels," *Child Development,* 31 (June, 1960), 377–85.

Haveman, Ernest and Patricia West. *They Went to College.* New York: Harcourt, 1952.

Havighurst, Robert J. and Bernice L. Neugarten. *Society and Education,* 2nd ed. Boston: Allyn and Bacon, 1962.

Heer, David M. "Dominance and the Working Wife," *Social Forces,* 36 (May, 1958), 341–47.

————. "Measurement and Bases of Family Power," *Marriage and Family Living,* 25 (1963), 133–39.

Henry, Andrew F. "Family Role Structure and Self Blame," *Social Forces,* 35 (October, 1956), 34–38.

Henry, J. "Docility, or Giving Teacher What She Wants," *Journal of Social Issues,* 2 (1955), 33–41.

————. "Spontaneity, Initiative, and Creativity in Suburban Classrooms," in G. D. Spindler (ed.), *Education and Culture.* New York: Holt, 1963, pp. 215–33.

Herskovits, Melville J. *The Myth of the Negro Past.* New York: Harper, 1941.

Herzog, John D. "Deliberate Instruction and Household Structure," *Harvard Educational Review,* 32 (Summer, 1962), 301–42.

Hess, Robert D. "The Socialization of Attitudes Toward Political Authority: Some Cross-National Comparisons," *International Social Science Journal,* 15 (1963), 542–59.

———— and David Easton. "The Child's Changing Image of the President," *Public Opinion Quarterly,* 24 (Winter, 1960), 632–44.

————and David Easton. "The Role of the Elementary School in Political Socialization," *School Review*, 70 (1962), 257–65.

———— and Judith Torney. *The Development of Political Attitudes in Children*. Chicago: Aldine, 1967.

Hilgard, Ernest R. *Theories of Learning*, 2nd ed. New York: Appleton, 1960.

Hoffman, L. M. "Father's Role in Family and Child's Peer Group Adjustment," *Merrill-Palmer Quarterly*, 7 (1961), 98–105.

Hollingshead, August. *Elmtown's Youth*. New York: Wiley, 1949.

Holmes, Henry W. "The Civic Education Project of Cambridge," *Phi Delta Kappan*, 33 (December, 1951), 168–71.

Holtzman, W. H. "Attitudes of College Men Toward Non-Segregation in Texas Schools," *Public Opinion Quarterly*, 20 (1956), 559–69.

Houn, Franklin W. *To Change a Nation*. New York: Free Press, 1961.

Hovland, C. I. "Reconciling Conflicting Results Derived from Experimental and Survey Studies of Attitude Change," *American Psychologist*, 14 (1959), 8–17.

Huitt, Ralph. "A Case Study in Senate Norms," in John C. Wahlke and Heinz Eulau (eds.), *Legislative Behavior*. Glencoe: Free Press, 1959, pp. 284–94.

Hyman, Herbert H. "Mass Media and Political Socialization: The Role of Patterns of Communications," in Lucian Pye (ed.), *Communications and Political Development*. Princeton: Princeton University Press, 1963, pp. 128–48.

————. *Political Socialization*. New York: Free Press, 1959.

Inglehart, Ronald. "An End of European Integration?" *American Political Science Review*, 61 (March, 1967), 98–105.

Jackson, J. and C. McGehee. "Group Structure and Role Behavior," *The Annals*, 361 (September, 1965), 130–40.

Jahoda, Gustav. "Children's Concepts of Nationality: A Critical Study of Piaget's Stages," *Child Development*, 35 (1964), 1081–92.

————. "Development of the Perception of Social Differences in Children from 6 to 10," *The British Journal of Educational Psychology*, 50 (1959), 159–75.

————. "The Development of Children's Ideas About Country and Nationality, Part I: The Conceptual Framework," *The*

British Journal of Educational Psychology, 33 (1963), 47–60.

————. "The Development of Children's Ideas About Country and Nationality, Part II: National Symbols and Themes," *The British Journal of Educational Psychology,* 33 (1963), 143–53.

Janowitz, Morris. *Sociology and the Military Establishment.* New York: Russel Sage Foundation, 1959.

Jennings, M. Kent. "Correlates of the Social Studies Curriculum: Grades 10–12," in Benjamin Cox and Byron Massialas (eds.), *Social Studies in the United States.* New York: Harcourt, 1967.

————. "Pre-Adult Orientations to Multiple Systems of Government," *Midwest Journal of Political Science,* 11 (August, 1967), 291–317.

———— and Richard G. Niemi. "The Transmission of Political Values from Parent to Child," *American Political Science Review,* 62 (March, 1968), 169–84.

Jones, Mary C. "A Study of Socialization Patterns at the High School Level," *Journal of Genetic Psychology,* 93 (September, 1958), 87–111.

Kagan, Jerome. "The Concept of Identification," *Psychological Review,* 65 (September, 1958), 296–305.

————. and Howard Moss. *Birth to Maturity.* New York: Praeger, 1963.

————. "The Stability of Passive and Dependent Behavior from Childhood Through Adulthood," *Child Development,* 31 (September, 1960), 577–91.

Kardiner, Abram and Lionel Ovesey. *The Mark of Oppression.* Cleveland: World, 1962.

Karlsson, George. "Political Attitudes Among Male Swedish Youth," *Acta Sociologica,* 3 (1958), 220–41.

Karon, Bertram P. *Negro Personality: A Rigorous Investigation of the Effects of Culture.* New York: Springer, 1958.

Kassof, Allen. *The Soviet Youth Program: Regimentation and Rebellion.* Cambridge: Harvard University Press, 1965.

Katz, Irwin. "Research on Public School Desegregation," *Integrated Education,* 4, 4 (1966), 14–24.

————. "Review of Evidence Relating to Effects of Desegregation on the Intellectual Performance of Negroes," *American Psychologist,* 19 (1964), 381–99.

———— and Lawrence Benjamin. "Effects of White Authoritarianism in Biracial Work Groups," *Journal of Abnormal and Social Psychology*, 61 (November, 1960), 448–56.

Key, V. O., Jr. *Public Opinion and American Democracy*. New York: Knopf, 1963.

Killian, Lewis and Charles Grigg. *Racial Crises in America*. Englewood Cliffs: Prentice-Hall, 1964.

Koff, D. and C. Von Der Muhl. "Political Socialization in East Africa," *Journal of Modern African Studies*, 5 (May, 1967), 13–52.

Konig, René. "Family and Authority: The German Father in 1955," *Sociological Review*, 5 (New Series, July, 1957), 107–27.

Kornberg, Allan and Norman Thomas. "The Political Socialization of National Legislative Elites in the United States and Canada," *Journal of Politics*, 27 (1965), 761–75.

Kornhauser, Arthur. "Changes in the Information and Attitudes of Students in an Economics Class," *Journal of Educational Research*, 22 (1930), 288–308.

Krug, Mark M. " 'Safe' Textbooks and Citizenship Education," *School Review*, 68 (1960), 463–80.

Kuroda, Yasumasa. "Agencies of Political Socialization and Political Change: Political Orientation of Japanese Law Students," *Human Organization*, 24 (1965), 328–31.

Kvaraceus, William C., et al. *Negro Self-Concept: Implication for School and Citizenship*. New York: McGraw-Hill, 1965.

Lambert, William W. and Wallace E. Lambert. *Social Psychology*. Englewood Cliffs: Prentice-Hall, 1964.

Lane, Robert E. "Fathers and Sons: Foundations of Political Belief," *American Sociological Review*, 24 (August, 1959), 502–11.

———. "Political Character and Political Analysis," in Heinz Eulau, Samuel Eldersveld, and Morris Janowitz (eds.), *Political Behavior*. Glencoe: Free Press, 1959, pp. 115–25.

———. *Political Ideology*. New York: Free Press, 1962.

———. *Political Life*. Glencoe: Free Press, 1959.

———. "The Need to Be Liked and the Anxious College Liberal," *The Annals*, 361 (1965), 71–80.

——— and David Sears. *Public Opinion*. Englewood Cliffs: Prentice-Hall, 1964.

Langdon, Frank. *Politics in Japan*. Boston: Little, Brown, 1967.

Langton, Kenneth P. *Civic Attitudes of Jamaican High School Students*. Cooperative Research Project, United States Department of Health, Education, and Welfare, 1965.

――――. "Political Partisanship and Political Socialization in Jamaica," *British Journal of Sociology*, 17 (December, 1966), 419–29.

LaPalombara, Joseph and Jerry B. Waters. "Values, Expectations, and Political Predispositions of Italian Youth," *Midwest Journal of Political Science*, 5 (1961), 39–58.

Lasswell, Harold D. "The Selective Effect of Personality on Political Participation," in R. Christie and M. Jahoda (eds.), *Studies in the Scope and Method of the Authoritarian Personality*. Glencoe: Free Press, 1954, pp. 197–266.

Lawson, Edwin D. "Development of Patriotism in Children—A Second Look," *Journal of Psychology*, 55 (1963), 279–86.

Lazarsfeld, Paul F., *et al.* "The Process of Opinion and Attitude Formation," in Paul F. Lazarsfeld and Morris Rosenberg (eds.), *The Language of Social Research*. Glencoe: Free Press, 1955, pp. 231–42.

Lehman, Irvin J. "Changes in Attitudes and Values Associated with College Attendance," *Journal of Educational Psychology*, 57 (April, 1966), 89–98.

Lerner, Daniel. *The Passing of Traditional Society*. Glencoe: Free Press, 1958.

Levin, Martin L. "Social Climates and Political Socialization," *Public Opinion Quarterly*, 25 (Winter, 1961), 596–606.

LeVine, Robert A. "Political Socialization and Cultural Change," in G. Geertz (ed.), *Old Societies and New Studies*. New York: Free Press, 1963, pp. 280–303.

――――. "The Role of the Family in Authority Systems: A Cross-Cultural Application of Stimulus-Generalization Theory," *Behavioral Science*, 5 (1960), 291–96.

Levy, Edwin. "Children's Behavior Under Stress and Its Relation to Training by Parents to Respond to Stress Situations," *Child Development*, 30 (1959), 307–24.

Lifton, Robert J. *Thought Reform and the Psychology of Totalism*. New York: Norton, 1961.

Lippitt, G. L. (ed.). "Training for Political Participation," *Journal of Social Issues*, 16 (1960), entire issue.

Lipset, Seymour Martin (ed.). *Student Politics, A Special Issue of the Comparative Education Review,* 10, 2 (1966), entire issue.

————. "The Political Behavior of University Students in Developing Nations," *Social and Economic Studies,* 14 (1965), 35–75.

Litt, Edgar. "Civic Education Norms and Political Indoctrination," *American Sociological Review,* 28 (February, 1963), 69–75.

Lunstrum, John P. "The Treatment of Controversial Issues in Social Studies Instruction," in Byron G. Massialas and Frederick R. Smith, (eds.), *New Challenges in the Social Studies.* Belmont, California: Wadsworth, 1965, pp. 121–47.

Lynes, Russell. *A Surfeit of Honey.* New York: Wiley, 1958.

Lynn, David B. "Sex Differences in Identification Development," *Sociometry,* 24 (December, 1961), 372–84.

Lynn, David and William Sawrey. "Effects of Father Absence on Norwegian Boys and Girls," *Journal of Abnormal and Social Psychology,* 19 (September, 1959), 258–62.

Maccoby, Eleanor E. "Choice of Variables in the Study of Socialization," *Sociometry,* 24 (December, 1961), 357–71.

————. Richard Mathews, and Anton Morton. "Youth and Political Change," *Public Opinion Quarterly,* 18 (Spring, 1954), 23–39.

Mainer, Robert E. "Attitude Change in Intergroup Programs," in H. H. Remmers (ed.), *Anti-Democratic Attitudes in American Schools.* Evanston: Northwestern University Press, 1963, pp. 122–54.

March, James. "Husband-Wife Interaction over Political Issues," *Public Opinion Quarterly,* 17 (Winter, 1953–1954), 461–70.

Martin, William E. and Stendler, Celia B. *Child Behavior and Development.* New York: Harcourt, 1959.

Marvick, Dwaine. "The Political Socialization of the American Negro," *The Annals,* 361 (September, 1965), 112–27.

Matthews, Donald R. *U. S. Senators and Their World.* New York: Knopf, 1960.

———— and James W. Prothro. *Negroes and the New Southern Politics.* New York: Harcourt, 1966.

McClelland, David. *The Achieving Society.* Princeton: Van Nostrand, 1961.

————, *et al.* "Obligations to Self and Society in the United

States and Germany," *Journal of Abnormal and Social Psychology*, 33 (1963), 107–19.

McClintock, Charles G. and Henry A. Turner. "The Impact of College upon Political Knowledge, Participation, and Values," *Human Relations*, 15 (May, 1962), 163–76.

McClosky, Herbert and Harold Dahlgren. "Primary Group Influence on Party Loyalty," *American Political Science Review*, 53 (September, 1959), 762.

———— and John H. Schaar. "Psychological Dimensions of Anomy," *American Sociological Review*, 30 (February, 1965), 14–40.

Mead, Margaret. "The Study of National Character," in Daniel Learner and Harold Lasswell (eds.), *The Policy Sciences*. Stanford: Stanford University Press, 1951, pp. 70–85.

Merriam, Charles E. *The Making of Citizens: A Comparative Study of Methods of Civic Training*. Chicago: University of Chicago Press, 1931.

Michael, John. "High School Climates and Plans for Entering College," *Public Opinion Quarterly*, 25 (Winter, 1961), 583–95.

Middleton, Russell and Snell, Putney. "Influences on the Political Beliefs of American College Students," *Politico*, 29 (1964), 484–92.

————. "Political Expression of Adolescent Rebellion," *American Journal of Sociology*, 68 (March, 1963), 527–35.

Milbrath, Lester W. *Political Participation*. Chicago: Rand McNally, 1965.

————. "Predispositions Toward Political Contention," *Western Political Quarterly*, 13 (March, 1960), 5–18.

Miller, David and Guy Swanson. *The Changing American Parent*. New York: Wiley, 1958.

Miller, Neal and John Dollard. *Social Learning and Imitation*. New Haven: Yale University Press, 1941.

Mischel, W. "Preference for Delayed Reinforcement: An Experimental Study of Cultural Observation," *Journal of Abnormal and Social Psychology*, 56 (1958), 57–61.

Mitchell, William C. *The American Policy*. Glencoe: Free Press, 1962.

————. *Sociological Analysis and Politics*. Englewood Cliffs: Prentice-Hall, 1967.

Moore, Joan W. "Social Deprivation and Advantage as Sources of Political Values," *Western Political Quarterly,* 15 (1962), 217–226.

Mosel, James N. "Communication Patterns and Political Socialization in Transitional Thailand," in Lucian Pye (ed.), *Communications and Political Development.* Princeton: Princeton University Press, 1963, pp. 184–228.

Moynihan, D. P. *The Negro Family.* U. S. Department of Labor, 1965.

Murdock, George E. "World Ethnographic Sample," in Frank W. Moore (ed.), *Readings in Cross-Cultural Methodology.* New Haven: Hraf Press, 1961, pp. 193–216.

Musgrove, F. A. "Uganda Secondary School as a Field of Culture Change," *Africa,* 22 (1952), 234–49.

Myrdal, Gunnar. *An American Dilemma.* New York: Harper, 1944.

Nash, John. "The Father in Contemporary Culture," *Culture Development,* 36 (1965), 261–97.

Neugarten, Bernice L. "Democracy of Childhood," in William Lloyd Warner, *et al.* (eds.), *Democracy in Jonesville.* New York: Harper, 1949, Chapter 5.

————. "Social Class and Friendship Among School Children," *The American Sociological Review,* 51 (January, 1946), 305–13.

Newcomb, Theodore M. "Persistence and Regression of Changed Attitudes: Long Range Studies," *Journal of Social Issues,* 19 (1963), 3–14.

————. *Personality and Social Change.* New York: Dryden Press, 1943.

————. "Student Peer Group Influence," in Robert Sutherland, *et al., Personality Factors on the College Campus.* Austin: Hogg Foundation, 1962, p. 69.

————. "The General Nature of Peer Group Influence," in Theodore M. Newcomb and Everett K. Wilson (eds.), *College Peer Groups.* Chicago: Aldine, 1966, pp. 2–6.

————, *et al. Persistence and Change: Bennington College and Its Students After Twenty-Five Years.* New York: Wiley, 1967.

Niemi, Richard. "Collecting Information about the Family: A Problem in Survey Methodology," in Frederick Frey and Jack Dennis (eds.), *Political Socialization: A Reader in Theory and Research.* Forthcoming.

Nogee, Philip and Levin, Murray. "Some Determinants of Political Attitudes among College Voters," *Public Opinion Quarterly*, 22 (Winter, 1958), 449–63.

Nordlinger, Eric. *The Working Class Tories*. Berkeley: University of California Press, 1968.

Ogburn, William and Nimkoff, Meyer. *Technology and the Changing Family*. Boston: Houghton Mifflin, 1955.

Orbell, John. "Protest Participation Among Negro College Students," *The American Political Science Review*, 61 (June, 1967), 446–56.

Orlansky, Harold. "Infant Care and Personality," *Psychological Bulletin*, 46 (January, 1949), 1–48.

Osgood, C. E. "Behavior Theory and the Social Sciences," in R. Young (ed.), *Approaches to the Study of Politics*. Evanston: Northwestern University Press, 1958. 217–44.

Pace, Robert C. "What Kind of Citizens Do College Graduates Become," *Journal of General Education*, 3 (April, 1949), 197–202.

Parsons, Talcott. *The Social System*. Glencoe: Free Press, 1951.

———— and Robert Bales. *Family Socialization and Interaction Process*. Glencoe: Free Press, 1965.

———— and Neil Smelser. *Economy and Society*. Glencoe: Free Press, 1956.

Patterson, Franklin. "Citizenship and the High School: Representative Current Practices," in Franklin Patterson, *et al.*, *The Adolescent Citizen*. New York: Free Press, 1960, Chapter 5.

Peck, Robert F. "Family Patterns Correlated with Adolescent Personality Structure," *Journal of Abnormal and Social Psychology*, 57 (November, 1958), 347–50.

Pettigrew, Thomas F. *A Profile of the American Negro*. Princeton: Van Nostrand, 1964.

Piaget, Jean and Anne-Marie Weil. "The Development in Children of the Idea of the Homeland and Relations with Other Countries," *International Social Science Bulletin*, 3 (1951), 561–78.

Pinner, Frank A. "Parental Overprotection and Political Distrust," *The Annals*, 361 (September, 1965), 58–70.

————. "Student Trade-Unionism in France, Belgium, and Holland: Anticipatory Socialization and Role-Seeking," *Sociology of Education*, 37 (1964), 177–99.

Plant, Walter P. "Changes in Intolerance and Authoritarianism for Sorority and Non-Sorority Women," *Journal of Psychology*, 68 (February, 1966), 79–83.

———. "Longitudinal Changes in Intolerance and Authoritarianism for Subjects Differing in Amounts of College Education over Four Years," *Genetic Psychology Monographs*, 72 (November, 1965), 247–87.

Prewitt, Kenneth. "Political Socialization and Leadership Selection," *The Annals*, 361 (1965), 96–111.

Price, Roy A. "Citizenship Studies in Syracuse," *Phi Delta Kappan*, 33 (December, 1951), 179–81.

Pye, Lucian W. "Communications and Civic Training in Transitional Societies," in Lucian Pye (ed.), *Communications and Political Development*. Princeton: Princeton University Press, 1963, pp. 124–27.

———. *Politics, Personality and Nation Building*. New Haven: Yale University Press, 1962.

———. "Political Modernization and Research on the Process of Political Socialization," *Items*, 13 (1959), 25–28.

———. "The Stages of Socialization: The Problem of Nation Building," in Joseph Fiszman, (ed.), *American Political Arena*. Boston: Little, Brown, 1966, pp. 84–87.

Quillen, I. James. "Government Oriented Courses in the Secondary School Curriculum," in Donald H. Riddle and Robert S. Cleary (eds.), *Political Science in the Social Studies*, 36 Yearbook, National Council for the Social Studies, 1966, pp. 245–72.

Remmers, H. H. and D. H. Radler. *The American Teenager*. New York: Bobbs-Merrill, 1962.

Riesman, David. *Faces in the Crowd*. New Haven: Yale University Press, 1952.

———. *The Lonely Crowd*. New Haven: Yale University Press, 1950.

Robinson, James A., et al. "Teaching with Inter-Nation Simulation and Case Studies," *American Political Science Review*, 60 (March, 1966), 53–65.

Rodnick, David. *Postwar Germans*. New Haven: Yale University Press, 1948.

Rokeach, Milton. *The Open and Closed Mind*. New York: Basic Books, 1960.

Rollins, James C. "Two Empirical Tests of a Parsonian Theory of Family Authority Patterns," *The Family Life Coordinator* (January–April, 1963), entire issue.

Rose, Arnold. "A Systematic Summary of Symbolic Interaction Theory," in Arnold Rose (ed.), *Human Behavior and Social Processes*. Boston: Houghton Mifflin, 1962, pp. 3–19.

Rose, Peter. "Student Opinion on the 1956 Presidential Election," *Public Opinion Quarterly*, 21 (1957), 371–76.

Rose, Richard. *Politics in England*. Boston: Little, Brown, 1964.

Rosenberg, Milton J. "An Analysis of Affective-Cognitive Consistency," in M. J. Rosenberg, *et al.* (eds.), *Attitude Organization and Change*. New Haven: Yale University Press, 1960, pp. 22–32.

Sanford, Nevitt (ed.). *The American College*. New York: Knopf, 1963.

Schaefer, E. "Converging Conceptual Models for Maternal Behavior and for Child Behavior," in J. C. Glidewell (ed.), *Parental Attitudes and Child Behavior*. Springfield, Illinois: Charles C. Thomas, 1961.

Schaffner, Bertram. *Fatherland: A Study of Authoritarianism in the German Family*. New York: Columbia University Press, 1948.

Schiff, L. F. "The Obedient Rebels: A Study of College Conversions to Conservatism," *Journal of Social Issues*, 20 (1964), 74–95.

Schlesinger, Benjamin. "A Survey of Methods Used to Study Decision Making in the Family," *The Family Life Coordinator*, 6 (January, 1962), 8–14.

Sclarew, Bruce H. "Relationship of Early Separation from Parents to Differences in Adjustment in Adolescent Boys and Girls," *Psychiatry*, 22 (November, 1959), 399–405.

Scott, Robert E. "Mexico: The Established Revolution," in Lucian W. Pye and Sidney Verba (eds.), *Political Culture and Political Development*. Princeton: Princeton University Press, 1965, pp. 347–71.

Seasholes, Bradbury. "Political Socialization of Negroes: Image Development of Self and Policy," in William C. Kraraceus, *et al.*, *Negro Self-Concept*. New York: McGraw-Hill, 1965, pp. 52–90.

Selvin, Hanan C. and Warren O. Hagstrom. "The Determinants

of Support for Civil Liberties," *British Journal of Sociology,* 11 (1960), 51–73.

Sewell, William H. "Some Recent Developments in Socialization Theory and Research," *The Annals,* 349 (September, 1963), 163–81.

Shaver, James P. "Reflective Thinking, Values, and Social Studies Textbooks," *School Review,* 73 (1965), 226–57.

Shick, Marvin and Albert Somit. "The Failure to Teach Political Activity," *American Behavioral Scientist,* 6 (January, 1963), 5–8.

Shils, Edward. "The Intellectuals in the Political Development of the New Nations," *World Politics,* 12 (April, 1960), 329–68.

Sigel, Roberta S. "An Exploration into Some Aspects of Political Socialization: School Children's Reaction to the Death of a President," in Martha Wolfenstein and Gilbert Kliman (eds.), *Children and the Death of a President.* Garden City: Doubleday, 1965, pp. 30–61.

———. "Image of a President: Some Insights into the Political Views of School Children," *American Political Science Review,* 62 (March, 1968), 216–26.

———. "Image of the American Presidency—Part II of an Exploration into Popular Views," *Midwest Journal of Political Science,* 40 (1966), 123–37.

Simon, Herbert. "Causal Ordering and Identifiability," in W. C. Hood and T. C. Koopmans, *Studies in Econometric Method.* New York: Wiley, 1953, pp. 49–74.

Skrzypek, Stanislaw. "The Political, Cultural, and Social Views of Yugoslav Youth," *Public Opinion Quarterly,* 29 (1965), 87–106.

Smith, M. G. *West Indian Family Structure.* Seattle: University of Washington Press, 1962.

Solien, Nancie L. "Household and Family in the Caribbean: Some Definitions and Concepts," *Social and Economic Studies,* 9 (March, 1960), 101–6.

Somit, Albert, *et al.* "The Effect of the Introductory Political Science Course on Student Attitudes Toward Political Participation," *American Political Science Review,* 52 (December, 1958), 1129–32.

Spiro, M. E. *Children of the Kibbutz*. Cambridge: Harvard University Press, 1958.

Stember, C. H. *Education and Attitude Change*. New York: Institute of Human Relations Press, 1961.

Stendler, Cecil B. *Children of Brasstown*. Urbana: Bureau of Research and Service of the College of Education, University of Illinois, 1949.

Stevenson, Harold W. and Edward C. Stuart. "A Developmental Study of Racial Awareness in Young Children," *Child Development*, 29 (1958), 399–409.

Stolz, Louis M. *Father Relations of War Born Children*. Stanford: Stanford University Press, 1954.

Stoodley, Bartlett. "Normative Attitudes of Filipino Youth Compared with German and American Youth," *American Sociological Review*, 22 (1957), 553–61.

Strauss, Murray A. "Conjugal Power Structure and Adolescent Personality," *Marriage and Family Living*, 24 (February, 1962), 17–25.

Teune, Henry. "The Learning of Integrative Habits," in Philip E. Jacob and James V. Toscano (eds.), *The Integration of Political Communities*. Philadelphia: Lippincott, 1964, pp. 247–82.

Tiller, P. O. "Father Absence and Personality Development of Children in Sailor Families," in N. Anderson (ed.), *Studies of the Family*, 2, Part II. Gottingen: Vanderhoeck and Ruprecht, 1957, pp. 115–37.

Thompson, Leonard M. *Politics in the Republic of South Africa*. Boston: Little, Brown, 1966.

Torgerson, Warren S. *Theory and Methods of Scaling*. New York: Wiley, 1958.

Ullman, Albert D. "Sociology and Character Education," in Franklin Patterson, *et al.* (eds.), *The Adolescent Citizen*. Glencoe: Free Press, 1960, pp. 206–23.

Verba, Sidney. "Comparative Political Culture," in Lucian W. Pye and Sidney Verba (eds.), *Political Culture and Political Development*. Princeton: Princeton University Press, 1965, pp. 512–60.

———. "Germany: The Remaking of Political Culture," in Lucian W. Pye and Sidney Verba (eds.), *Political Culture and Political Development*. Princeton: Princeton University Press, 1965, 154–68.

————. *Small Groups and Political Behavior*. Princeton: Princeton University Press, 1961.

Ward, Robert E. "Japan: The Continuity of Modernization," in Lucian W. Pye and Sidney Verba (eds.), *Political Culture and Political Development*. Princeton: Princeton University Press, 1965, pp. 44–53.

Wasby, Stephen L. "The Impact of the Family on Politics: An Essay and Review of the Literature," *Family Life Coordinator*, 15 (January, 1966), 3–23.

Weiler, Hans N. (ed.). *Education and Politics in Nigeria*. Freiburg in Briesgau: Rombach, 1964.

Weiser, John and James Hayes. "Democratic Attitudes of Teachers and Prospective Teachers," *Phi Delta Kappan*, 47 (May, 1966), 470–81.

Werner, F. "Acculturation and Milieu Therapy in Student Transition," in G. Spindler (ed.), *Education and Culture—Anthropological Approaches*. New York: Holt, 1963, pp. 259–67.

Whiting, John M. "Resource Mediation and Learning by Identification," in Ira Iscoe and Harold Stevenson, *Personality and Development in Children*. Austin: University of Texas Press, 1960, pp. 112–26.

———— and Irving L. Child. *Child Training and Personality: A Cross Cultural Study*. New Haven: Yale University Press, 1963.

Wilder, Emilia. "Impact of Poland's Stabilization on Its Youth," *Public Opinion Quarterly*, 28 (1964), 447–52.

Wilkinson, R. *Gentlemanly Power: British Leadership and the Public School Tradition*. London and New York: Oxford University Press, 1964.

Willis, R. H. "Political and Child-Rearing Attitudes in Sweden," *Journal of Abnormal and Social Psychology*, 53 (1956), 74–77.

Wilson, Alan B. "Residential Segregation of Social Classes and Aspirations of High School Boys," *American Sociological Review*, 24 (December, 1959), 836–45.

Wilson, Everett K. "The Entering Student: Attributes and Agents of Change," in Theodore M. Newcomb and Everett K. Wilson (ed.), *College Peer Groups*. Chicago: Aldine, 1966, pp. 84–87.

Winch, Robert F. *Identification and Its Familial Determinants*. New York: Bobbs-Merrill, 1962.

Wolgast, Elizabeth. "Do Husbands or Wives Make the Purchasing Decisions?" *The Journal of Marketing*, 23 (October, 1958), 151–58.

Wright, S. "The Interpretation of Multivariate Systems," in O. Kempthrone, *et al.*, *Statistics and Mathematics in Biology*. Ames: Iowa State College Press, 1954, pp. 11–33.

Wrong, Dennis H. "The Oversocialized Conception of Man in Modern Sociology," *American Sociological Review*, 26 (1961), 183–93.

Wylie, Lawrence. *Village in the Vaucluse*, 2nd ed. New York: Harper, 1964.

Yu, T. C. *Mass Persuasion in Communist China*. New York: Praeger, 1964.

Zeigler, Harmon. *The Political World of the High School Teacher*. Eugene: The Center for the Advanced Study of Educational Administration, University of Oregon, 1966.

Ziblatt, David. "High School Extra-Curricular Activities and Political Socialization," *The Annals*, 361 (September, 1965), 21–31.

Unpublished Materials

Aberbach, Joel D. "The Political Implications of Race: An Analysis of the Roots and Consequences of Political Alienation." Ph.D. dissertation, Yale University, Department of Political Science, 1966.

Abramson, Paul. "Political Socialization of English Schoolboys." Ph.D. dissertation, University of California, Berkeley, Department of Political Science, 1966.

Appell, John S. and Bert A. Rockman. "Political Socialization: Stability and Change of Integenerational Effects over the Life as They Affect Partisan Identification." M.A. thesis, University of Michigan, 1966, pp. 16–46.

Converse, Philip E. "Attitudes and Non-Attitudes: Continuation of a Dialogue." Unpublished paper, Survey Research Center, University of Michigan, February, 1963.

Dennis, Jack. "A Working Paper on Nine Basic Problems of Political Socialization Research Relevant to the Study of the Role of the School in Civic Education." Theory and Research Working Committee on Political Socialization, Lincoln Filene

Center for Citizenship and Public Affairs, Tufts University, Medford, Massachusetts, 1965.

————. "Recent Research on Political Socialization: A Bibliography of Published, Forthcoming, and Unpublished Works, Theses, and Dissertations and a Survey of Projects in Progress." Prepared for the Theory and Research Working Committee on Political Socialization of the Council on Civic Education, Lincoln Filene Center for Citizenship and Public Affairs, Tufts University, Medford, Massachusetts, 1967.

Devereux, Edward C. Jr. "Children of Democracy: On the Consequences for Children of Varying Patterns of Family Authority in the United States and West Germany." Summary of a paper presented to the 7th International Seminar on Family Research, Washington, D. C., September, 1962.

Duke, James T. "Equalitarianism Among Emergent Elites in a New Nation." Ph.D. dissertation, University of California, Los Angeles, 1963.

Frey, Frederick W. "Socialization to National Identification: Turkish Peasants." Paper delivered at the American Political Science Association Meeting, New York, September, 1966.

Garrison, Charles. "The Introductory Political Science Course as an Agent of Political Socialization." Ph.D. dissertation, University of Oregon, 1966.

Heggan, Jon. "Political Socialization in the Educational System of Colombia." Ph.D. dissertation in progress, University of Illinois, 1966.

Herzog, John D. "Additional Parameters for Educational Planners: Some Thoughts from Research in Barbados." Harvard University, School of Education, 1964.

Hess, Robert D. "Models of Political Socialization." A paper prepared for the Theory and Research Working Committee on Political Socialization of the Council on Civic Education, Lincoln Filene Center for Citizenship and Public Affairs, Tufts University, Medford, Massachusetts, May, 1965.

Inglehart, Ronald. "The Socialization of Europeans: Nation-Building in Western Europe." Ph.D. dissertation, University of Chicago, Department of Political Science, 1966.

Jaros, D. "Explorations into Children's Orientations to Political Authority." Paper presented at the Midwest Political Science Conference, 1966.

Kantor, S. and D. Brown. "Changes in Attitude and Behavior as a Function of Higher Education." Paper presented at the Midwestern Psychological Association, 1965.

Niemi, Richard G. "A Methodological Study of Political Socialization in the Family." Ph.D. dissertation, University of Michigan, Department of Political Science, 1967.

Patrick, John J. "Political Socialization of American Youth: A Review of Research with Implications for Secondary School Social Studies." High School Curriculum Center in Government, University of Indiana, Bloomington, 1967.

Reading, Reid. "A Cross-Cultural Study of Political Socialization: Colombia and the United States." Ph.D. dissertation, University of Wisconsin, Department of Political Science, 1967.

Sigel, Roberta. "Political Socialization: Some Reactions on Current Approaches and Conceptualizations." A paper presented at the Annual Meeting of the American Political Science Association, New York, 1966.

Stokes, Donald E. "Ideological Competition of British Parties." Paper presented at the Annual Meeting of the American Political Science Association, Chicago, 1964.

Verba, Sidney. "The Comparative Study of Political Socialization." A paper presented at the Annual Meeting of the American Political Science Association, Chicago, September, 1964.

INDEX